William Patrick Patterson

TAKING WITH
THE LEFT HAND

Enneagram Craze,
People of the Bookmark,
& The Mouravieff 'Phenomenon'

William Patrick Patterson

Edited by Barbara Allen Patterson

Arete Communications, Publishers
Fairfax, California

Taking with the Left Hand
Enneagram Craze, People of the Bookmark,
& The Mouravieff 'Phenomenon'
© 1998 by William Patrick Patterson
All rights reserved

The essays in this book have been expanded from articles which first
appeared in *Telos*, the journal of inquiry into self-transformation in the
contemporary world. *Telos* explores the ideas and perspectives of the
Fourth Way teaching.

Design by WordPlay Consulting, Berkeley, CA

Library of Congress Catalog Number is 98-70064
Patterson, William Patrick
Taking with the Left Hand
Enneagram Craze, Bookmark People, & The Mouravieff 'Phenomenon'
Bibliography: Includes notes, references, and index
1. Spiritual Deflection and Distortion
2. Fellowship of Friends
3. Enneagram
4. Boris Mouravieff
5. Esoteric Christianity
5. Fourth Way
6. G. I. Gurdjieff

First printing 1998

ISBN: 1-879514-10-9

Arete Communications, Box 58, 773 Center Boulevard
Fairfax, California 94978-0058

email: Telos9@aol.com
Web Site: http://members.aol.com/Telos9

Printed in Canada

Dedication

For Prince Ozay,
the Great Charvaka

Other Books by the Author

Acknowledgments

It is one thing to write a book and quite another to prepare it for publication. The first one does alone, for the second one must rely on the voluntary effort of many others without whose skills this book would not stand as it does. In this regard, I would like to thank my wife Barbara, Henry Korman and Teresa Sanchez-Adams for the quality of their interest, professional skills and unstinting labor. I thank, too, those who have read the manuscript in its various stages. These are J. Walter Driscoll, Philip Goldsmith, and Steve Heath.

Contents

Prologue

I N TIME EVERYTHING CHANGES. WE *THINK* WE KNOW THAT. YET SO OFTEN OUR EXPECTATIONS AND ACTIONS are otherwise. The idea, the impulse, we begin with so often ends up its opposite...and we are surprised, shocked. How could this happen?

G. I. Gurdjieff, the extraordinary man who brought the ancient teaching of the Fourth Way to the West, knew better. His understanding went beyond the ordinary intellectual knowing. He not only expected change, he prepared for it. He knew that—as with all things in time—the sacred teaching he brought must come to moments, intervals, where counter currents could deflect it from its original impulse. To maintain the integrity of its movement, the dispersive influences of the ordinary world would have to be resisted and rightly absorbed.

Gurdjieff's aim was to establish the teaching, reformulated for our time, in the West. It was, he said, "completely unknown up to the present time." A key tenet of the teaching was that one learned to use ordinary life, not avoid or retreat from it. The uncertainty, negativity and suffering of ordinary life would be used to develop one's genuine individuality. The abnormal growth of egotism and powers of destruction had become so maleficent that only conscious resistance could restore the necessary balance and order. As Gurdjieff declared—long before it became fashionable to say such things—*Unless the 'wisdom' of the East and the 'energy' of the West could be harnessed and used harmoniously, the world would be destroyed.*

Gurdjieff went to Russia in 1912 to begin establishing the teaching. His intention was to create a school through which the teaching would be promulgated. But the ensuing Russian Revolution of 1917 made that impossible. After a number of attempts in Tiflis, Constantinople, Berlin and London, Gurdjieff finally succeeded in establishing his Institute for the Harmonious Development of Man in France in 1921.

At that time the world was just reconfiguring itself based on the outcome of World War I, "the war to end all wars," as it was called, and the success of Marxism in Russia (which he saw as "satanic"). All eyes were on Europe and America, but Gurdjieff looked only toward America. A day would come, he predicted, when the Eastern world would again rise to a position of world importance and become a threat to the momentarily all-powerful, all-influential new culture of the Western world, which would be dominated by America—a very strong but very young country. It was essential that the teaching be brought to America, and so in January 1924 he and a group of students visited New York City, Bos-

8

ton, and Philadelphia, giving demonstrations and performing sacred dances. Returning to France, Gurdjieff left behind A. R. Orage, the noted English editor and literary critic, to establish the teaching.

The time looked exceedingly propitious. That summer, however, came an immense shock. A serious auto accident put Gurdjieff in a coma. Recovering, he realized the Institute could not develop and train a sufficient cadre of "helper-instructors" quickly enough, and so he formally closed it. Now, how would he go about establishing the teaching?

By the year's end, the answer came. If he could not establish the teaching in his own time, he would send it into a future time. But how to safeguard its integrity, its momentum? Powerful counter currents were inevitable, each carrying the threat of a descending deflection, a diminution and distortion of the teaching. Ingeniously, Gurdjieff decided to create a *Legominism*, an esoteric vehicle for transmitting genuine knowledge to remote generations. The Sphinx, the Great Pyramid, Chartres, chess, and the tarot are all examples of *Legominisms*. Though he was the consummate man of action, one who abhorred what he called the "bon ton literary language," Gurdjieff forced himself to become an author.

His *Legominism* was a series of three books entitled *All and Everything*, which contain the whole of his esoteric teaching, as much of it as can be set down in this medium, and which, in accord with his intention, most people find virtually unreadable. Gurdjieff well understood that unless one has been properly prepared to receive higher knowledge, it means nothing or, worse, becomes its opposite—higher knowledge used in the service of egotistic ends.

To the surprise of no one who has studied and practiced the teaching, the anticipated deflections and distortions have occurred. But they have been manifested at the margins of the teaching, where it is in contact with the ordinary world. These deflections, however noxious, have had their use in that they have served to test a seeker's sincerity, intent, and discrimination. Previously, they have simply been ignored. For any challenge not only brings them more attention but lends a certain legitimacy in the public mind. And yet a time comes when so much has been taken with the left hand, as it were, that the esoteric has been so obscured and confused with the psychological, that a counter influence must be set in motion to provide a means of discrimination.

There have been too many deflections to attempt a discussion of all of them, but three will serve as illustrations:

1. *"Ennea-typers,"* those who have stripped the enneagram, a principal symbol of the Fourth Way, from Gurdjieff's teaching and used it as a secular personality tool;

2. *People of the Bookmark*, a.k.a. Robert Burton's Fellowship of Friends, and his derivatives, who falsely represent themselves as having a connection with the Fourth Way;

3. *Boris Mouravieff/Robin Amis* who attempt to co-opt the teaching and assimilate it into an established religion.

My personal acquaintance with those to be mentioned in this study is slight to nonexistent. It is not the people but their ideas and actions relative to the Fourth Way teaching that will be scrutinized. At the outset let it be stated that no ill will is intended. Yet one would be naive to believe that it will not be taken so, no matter how serious the attempt to discuss ideas and actions dispassionately.

I first came in contact with Helen Palmer, the Berkeley psychic, or "intuitive," as she prefers to be called, some ten years ago when she was speaking about her first book on the enneagram at a bookstore near my home. I was interested in how she knew Lord John Pentland, my teacher in the Gurdjieff work, for she had dedicated the book to "Sir John Pentland for his counsel and friendship." The dedication implied that her book had his stamp of approval, which, given his long-standing effort to preserve the teaching from any popularization, I thought odd. There was no authenticating the dedication as he had died some four years earlier, but oddly, Mrs. Palmer referred to him as *Sir* John Pentland, a lesser title by which he was never known. Everyone who knew him always addressed him and spoke of him as *Lord* Pentland. Was it a misprint? I wanted to find out.

During the discussion after Mrs. Palmer's talk, I asked her whether she indeed knew "Sir Pentland" well. Intense and articulate, she quickly recounted how he had called her in the early 1970s, saying he had read her psychic predictions in *Ramparts* magazine and wanted to meet her.

They had lunch shortly afterward during which Palmer said she told him of taking a class in the enneagram of personality fixations taught by the Chilean psychiatrist and Gestalt therapist Claudio Naranjo who, in turn, had learned it from Oscar Ichazo, the Bolivian esotericist. Pentland, she recounted, told her that little of real value could come from studying the symbol divorced as it was from the Fourth Way teaching of which it was one of the principal symbols. Rather than continue her studies, he advised her to enter the teaching. Palmer said she refused.

"Do you think," I asked, "that he would have approved your publishing a book on the enneagram?"

"No," she admitted, not missing a beat, "he probably wouldn't have."

My question was answered, and I saw no need to embarrass her in asking about the "Sir Pentland" dedication.

What I know of Robert Earl Burton is largely learned through newspaper accounts and personal contacts with his former students. The founder of The Fellowship of Friends with its satellite Gurdjieff-Ouspensky Centres set up around the world, Burton claims that his is a school of the Fourth Way. That Burton's only teacher was a faux-Gurdjieffian, having no connection to the teaching, and that he bases his teaching on Ouspensky, a pupil of Gurdjieff's, and not Gurdjieff himself, is apparently of no serious concern to him or his students. They are sometimes known as the "People of the Bookmark," because Burton has them stuff oversized bookmarks advertising Gurdjieff-Ouspensky Centres in all Fourth Way books.

Though I never met Burton, I did meet a man who was a member of his inner circle and who was present when Lord Pentland visited Burton. The film version of *Meetings with Remarkable Men* had been released and Burton had his students passing out flyers for Burton's centers to film-goers. Burton believed Pentland was coming to hand over his students to him because he had recognized Burton's "higher development"—Burton claims his is the highest consciousness man can attain. Burton even made a bet to this effect with several of his own students. In fact, Lord Pentland was coming to ask Burton to make a sizable contribution to the film inasmuch as he was falsely profiting by it. Upon Pentland's arrival, Burton presented him with an expensive sleeping pillow. This was Burton's idea of an esoteric joke. Several of Burton's close students joined the two men for dinner. "Watching the two of them together, there was just no question of which man was awake and which asleep," the former Burton student told me, "and I left the next day to become a student of Lord Pentland's."

I met a number of Burton's former students several summers ago while making a cross-county trip to promote a book. Following a talk in Missoula, Montana, a couple came back with my wife and me to our camp site. The man had been with Burton fifteen years, the woman eighteen. Disillusioned, but not as hurt or as angry as many we had encountered, they were trying to put the best face on their "Fellowship experience." They had learned something, they insisted, it hadn't been all bad. The continuing scandals and lawsuits against Burton by former students had forced them to leave. But they still felt he was teaching the Fourth Way, though they had no other experience of it to inform their judgment. Sitting by the campfire, watching their faces as they tried to make sense of it all, I wondered how much Burton actually did know, and so on my return I read his book and saw the truth of the matter.

The name "Boris Mouravieff" meant little to me. All I knew was that he was a friend of Ouspensky and had a strong animus toward Gurdjieff but nevertheless was enamored of the teaching. This wasn't unusual. Often Gurdjieff's method of teaching was to "step on corns," that is, make people aware of their self-love and vanity. It was only when I came across an article in *Gnosis* magazine entitled "Mouravieff and The Secret of The Source: Why was Gurdjieff's System revealed only in fragments?" that I gave any serious thought to what he and those who have been influenced by him represented. It began with the article's first paragraph:

> The subtitle of Ouspensky's book *In Search of the Miraculous*—the main text of the System known as the Fourth Way—is *Fragments of an Unknown Teaching*. But the real question is, why was the System only available in fragmentary form, and why are only fragments of the System available today, over seventy years after it was introduced?

The idea that Ouspensky's book, great as it is, is "the main text" of the teaching is simply not true. Ouspensky, as is well known, was a pupil of G. I. Gurdjieff, never his teacher. Ouspensky's book is an objective report of the teaching as Gurdjieff presented it during his Russian period (1912-1919).

The main text of the Fourth Way is Gurdjieff's *All and Everything*, the *First Series*, which has been available since 1949, the same year Ouspensky's book was published. The *Second Series* was published in 1963, and the *Third Series*, the conclusion of Gurdjieff's *Legominism*, was published in 1975.

From this alone one is left to conclude that either the author has made a fundamental mistake, something akin to saying that Clement's *Stromata* is the main text of Christianity, or he is intentionally setting up a straw argument. But if so, why?

Then there is the issue of the teaching being fragmentary, that is, incomplete. But Gurdjieff said the Fourth Way was "completely self-supporting," and so how can it at the same time be fragmentary? That the teaching is both fragmentary and not fragmentary is taken up in the section on "The Mouravieff 'Phenomenon'." It might be noted here, however, that Mouravieff's conventional "either yes-or-no" mindset leads him to the fundamental misunderstanding that the teaching is deficient and defective, an idea which his latter-day followers embrace with no more sophistication.

Later, I learned that the author of the *Gnosis* article was Robin Amis, the publisher and editor of the English version of Mouravieff's writings and founder and director of an institute to promote Mouravieff's viewpoint. It was then I realized why Amis would so misrepresent the Fourth Way and Gurdjieff. This was disappointing, since differences of viewpoint, honestly declared, can often lead to a deeper perspective.

My next encounter with Boris Mouravieff took place while researching my book, *Struggle of the Magicians*, which is centered on Gurdjieff's relationship with his students Ouspensky, Orage, and Bennett. I discovered that an English translation of Mouravieff's three-volume study *Gnosis*, first published in 1961 and out-of-print since 1966, had been published. It was most amazing to read. Mouravieff had simply picked up Gurdjieff's teaching and pasted it into the context of Eastern Orthodox Christianity. Such audacity was difficult to believe, as was the possibility that some people would take this seriously. The quality of writing alone, the consciousness and thinking, was not up to Ouspensky's level, much less Gurdjieff's. It should be remarked here that no criticism is intended in regard to Eastern Orthodox Christianity, which is highly respected. The focus is simply on Mouravieff's fundamental misunderstanding.

Gurdjieff was quite explicit in differentiating the Fourth Way from other teachings, but nevertheless Mouravieff insisted that the origin of the Fourth Way lies in the Eastern Orthodox Church. Interestingly, many exponents of other teachings, such as Sufism, the Kabbalah, even Theosophy, have also claimed the Fourth Way as their own. Why this interest in appropriating the teaching? What does it possess that so attracts them? One can only assume it somehow offers what their own teachings lack.

"The teaching whose theory is here being set out," Ouspensky reports Gurdjieff saying in *In Search of the Miraculous*, "is completely self-supporting and independent of other lines and it has been completely unknown up to the present time."

Completely self-supporting. Independent. Completely unknown. The words are strong, unequivocal. Their meaning is not subject to interpretation.

What seems to have really confused Mouravieff was that Gurdjieff also said—when asked what relationship the Fourth Way had to Christianity—that "if you like, it is esoteric Christianity."

Gurdjieff's answer, seemingly so direct, is multidimensional. That is, he speaks from two levels simultaneously. The answer on the first level is "yes," on the second, "no."

What Mouravieff missed are the operative words which modify Gurdjieff's answer—"if you like." In other words, taking into account the questioner's understanding, and his frame of reference, the Fourth Way is most analogous to Christianity; analogous, however, not to the public and preached version, whether Eastern or Latin, but to the esoteric version—that which enables one to live the precepts of Christ, not just speak them.

The word "esoteric" has a very special meaning for Gurdjieff. Every religion, he said, has two parts, one of which "becomes common knowledge and in the course of time is distorted and departs from the original. The other part teaches how to do what the first part teaches." This is the "yes" part of his answer.

But then he adds the "no" declaring that "The Christian church, the Christian form of worship, was not invented by the fathers of the church. It was all taken in ready-made form from Egypt, only not the Egypt that we know but from one which we do not know....It will seem strange to many people when I say that this prehistoric Egypt was Christian many thousands of years before the birth of Christ, that is to say, that its religion was composed of the same principles and ideas that constitute true Christianity."

How can we know this is true?

We can't.

However, what we can say irrefutably is that this is what Mr. Gurdjieff said.

Who then is this man George Ivanovitch Gurdjieff? And how could he make such far-reaching statements? How could he know?

While the scale of this question lies well beyond the range of the present book, Gurdjieff's identity, and how he could know, will be a major theme of my forthcoming book, *Law of the Sun, Law of the Moon*.

For Mouravieff, of course, there is no doubt that Gurdjieff is wrong. His argument is given in full here in Part III, along with its refutation, point-by-point, where it can be seen that Gurdjieff and his language is multidimensional, Mouravieff's understanding linear and literal. Never having been a student of Gurdjieff's, or initiated into his teaching, Mouravieff interprets and judges from, at best, an exoteric point of view. As Philip Sherrard, the highly regarded Christian intellectual, has pointed out: "If a man merely 'thinks' of the Truth with his mind, then all his logic is useless to him because he starts with an initial fallacy, the fallacy that the Truth can be attained by the unaided processes of human thought." This fallacy he calls "the philosophical mentality."

Philosophical mentality...these words so characterized Mouravieff that when his name came up thereafter I paid no attention. Then I was given an article Mouravieff had written about Gurdjieff, Ouspensky, and the teaching. The article was in French, so I had it translated. I was amazed to find that Mouravieff had gone well beyond the accusations he made in his book. I thought about writing an essay which would point out the flaws in his argument but decided against it as the article had not been given wide circulation. Further, and more importantly, to take Mouravieff seriously would give his views a platform. Better to let it die.

Mouravieff played no more part in my thinking until several years ago when I attended a conference at Bognor Regis in England. There, by chance, I had dinner with Robin Amis. A former advertising creative director, Amis is Mouravieff's publisher and editor and author of the article quoted earlier. Nothing of any import was exchanged. Though he was a bit guarded, I found him a good-natured, pleasant enough fellow. It was clear that were Mouravieff's views not at issue we would have got on well enough.

I was to speak that evening, he on the following day. During my talk, which focused on Gurdjieff's mission and his identity, I asked Amis to respond in his talk to Gurdjieff's direct statements concerning the source of the

Fourth Way teaching, which I then stated. He did not, and, while making the same claims as Mouravieff once did, provided no evidence, only hearsay and labored interpretation.

That would have been the end of it. But then I learned Amis had Mouravieff's essay translated into English and published it as a monograph. The seriousness of Mouravieff's misunderstanding and that of his latter-day followers demanded a refutation. With many misgivings, and only after a great deal of pondering, I decided to do so. My only qualification is my appreciation for what I have been given. I speak for myself only. While Lord Pentland strove always to preserve the teaching in its original form, he did not often involve himself in countering the ideas and -isms of the ordinary world. For argument so often only serves to harden and, in some sense, give credence to or legitimize, that which one is standing against. The Mouravieffs, the ennea-typers and the faux-Gurdjieffians, of course, have their place. Today's need is only to discriminate their correct place.

In the words of Gurdjieff:

> Pseudo-esoteric systems also play their part in the work and activities of esoteric circles. Namely, they are the intermediaries between humanity which is entirely immersed in the materialistic life and schools which are interested in the education of a certain number of people, as much for the purposes of their own existences as for the purposes of the work of a *cosmic* character which they may be carrying out. The very idea of esotericism, the idea of initiation, reaches people in most cases through pseudo-esoteric systems and schools; and if there were not these pseudo-esoteric schools the vast majority of humanity would have no possibility whatever of hearing and learning of the existence of anything greater than life because the truth in its pure form would be inaccessible for them. By reason of the many characteristics of man's being, particularly of the contemporary being, truth can only come to people *in the form of a lie*—only in this form are they able to accept it; only in this

form are they able to digest and assimilate it. Truth unde-
filed would be, for them, indigestible food.

In a time as psychologized and spiritually confused as
ours—"an empty and abortive interval," Gurdjieff called
it—what follows may provide a needed shock for those
still in genuine search. Δ

—William Patrick Patterson
San Anselmo, California

Part I

How the Enneagram Came to Market

The ancient esoteric teaching of the Fourth Way, reformulated for our time, was first introduced by G. I. Gurdjieff in Russia circa 1915. The teaching, Mr. Gurdjieff said, was "completely self-supporting and independent of other lines and it has been completely unknown up to the present time...[and the enneagram] is one of its principal symbols." In later discussions it was illustrated how the enneagram could be used to understand the relationship and transformation of the three foods (air, physical food, and impressions) within the body for the purposes of evolution and connection with higher being-bodies. The enneagram, he said, was "the fundamental hieroglyph of a universal language which has as many different meanings as there are levels of men." As a principal symbol of the teaching, it could not be understood or used appropriately outside the teaching. Said Gurdjieff, "The knowledge of the enneagram has for a very long time been preserved in secret and if it now is, so to speak, made available to all, it is only in an incomplete and theoretical form of which nobody could make any practical use without instruction from a man who knows."

The existence of the enneagram was first made widely known with the publication of P. D. Ouspensky's In Search of the Miraculous *in 1949. The application of the symbol to "personality fixations" was first introduced by Oscar Ichazo. Through Ichazo, Dr. Claudio Naranjo, a specialist in human typology, learned of what might be called "the personality enneagram" in 1969. Naranjo codified it into a system and, on his own accord, began to teach it to others with the proviso that they keep it a secret. This, of course, was naive. Interest in the enneagram, as applied to human typology or personality fixations, built steadily over the years but finally "came to market" in the late 1980s with the publication of numerous books on the personality enneagram.*

"I'VE TAUGHT THE ENNEAGRAM IN ADDICTION AND RECOVERY CENTERS, I'VE TAUGHT IT IN DANCE halls, I've taught it in high schools, and in business settings," said Helen Palmer. And taught it she certainly has, traveling the world giving lectures, workshops and corporate consultations, as well as teaching at her own 'school' in Berkeley. "The psychotherapists want it as a very useful, hot tool to work with normal, high-functioning people," said Mrs. Palmer. "Business consultants love it because it deeply facilitates conflict resolution. It really helps in negotiation and especially in team building." Her indefatigable crusading, unquestionable certainty in regard to the enneagram, and her three books on the subject—her first sold over 200,000 copies—have given her in the minds of many in what is called the enneagram community the title, "the mother of the personality enneagram."

And Mrs. Palmer is just one of the many who are pro-
pelling the enneagram movement. Jesuits, frocked and
defrocked, therapists, New Agers, human potential and
business consultants have all now published enneagram
books. Enneagram associations have been formed. There
are tapes, videos, study groups, certification courses,
retreats and workshops galore, even movie reviews—
Thelma and Louise is really a story of point nines and
counter-phobic point sixes; Clint Eastwood in *Dirty
Harry* is a point eight. Newsletters and monthly newspa-
pers have also sprung up running articles such as "The
Ennea-style," which features an analysis of how clothing
relates to various personalities of the enneagram. Point
ones, for example, "dress to repress," while point twos
"dress to effect," and so forth, until nine is reached where
the dressing is "dress to dress." Meanwhile, in business,
human resources people use the enneagram as a hiring
tool and, according to *Newsweek,* the CIA uses it to train
its agents. Some Hollywood and TV scriptwriters are
building their plots around it. The First International
Enneagram Conference held at prestigious Stanford University several years ago drew some 1,600 attendees.
Clearly, this is *the time of the enneagram.*

This personality enneagram—human typology or personality fixations as applied to the enneagram—is now
well-known in the areas of self-help, human resources,
therapy, and certain fringe spiritual groups. Its success
has brought its detractors, one of whom, the man commonly agreed to be "the father of the personality enneagram," Dr. Claudio Naranjo, said, "...the questionable
ethics of the earliest teachers has had cultural consequences, for I see the movement as pervaded by a combination of greed and arrogance and by great disrespect
toward the sources of the knowledge to the extent of insinuating that the tradition is a myth." Oscar Ichazo, known
to contemporary enneagrammers as the grandfather of the

23

personality enneagram, said, "Concretely speaking the enneagram authors start from the point of a 'belief,' which they make into a 'dogma,' because they accept it irrationally and in full without any analysis or criticism as if it would be a divine truth, unquestionable and final. They appoint an 'old Sufi' theory or whatever as their basis to elaborate scientific propositions. The work of the enneagram authors is plainly unscientific and without rational foundation, because it is based on dogmatic formulations." Ichazo is saying that Palmer, Naranjo and others do not know the source or real basis of the enneagram, the root series of principles upon which it operates, but instead take the enneagram as a given, ascribing its source to Sufis who, with a few come-lately exceptions, take no interest in it as it is not part of their teaching. Ichazo declared: "I know Sufism extensively—I've practiced traditional zhikr, prayer, meditation—and I know realized Sufi sheiks. It is not part of their theoretical framework. They couldn't care less about the Enneagon [Ichazo's name for the enneagram]."

Although born sixteen years after Gurdjieff first made the enneagram known, Oscar Ichazo nevertheless claims himself as the source of the enneagram or, as he would have it, enneagon. That cannot be true, but certainly he is responsible for introducing what might be called the "contemporary" enneagram. What is known of Ichazo is only what he has written or told others about himself and so its veracity is without witness. Sometimes the accounts differ. This is what he says: Born in 1931 in Bolivia, his father was a military officer and so his early years were spent at a military installation. By the age of six he was having periodic cataleptic attacks every few days in which he would become very rigid and frightened. To cure himself, at the age of thirteen, he took the drug ayahuasca (yaje) made, interestingly enough in terms of later events, from a vine which grows around trees in the Amazonian forests. More than once he says he had an out-of-body experience which allowed him "to experience the unity of matter." He went on to study yoga, hypnosis, Theosophy, Hindu philosophy, Pythagoras, Plato, Plotinus and the Kabbalah.

Then in La Paz in 1950, at the age of nineteen, he met a European businessman who gave him copies of Ouspensky's *In Search of the Miraculous* and *Tertium Organum.* The man told Ichazo of a study group in Buenos Aires to which he belonged and invited him to join. (Ichazo first said he spent four years with the group, later two years, then one year. In his early description, it was a Fourth Way group, in a later account it is undefined.) Upon his arrival in Buenos Aires, Ichazo was told to rent a large apartment for the group where they could work. He was to serve them while they worked, making coffee and so forth. He didn't live at the apartment, but in a hut on the outskirts of the city. The group passed him through a number of experiments or initiations, one of which was to sit in a lotus position on a post until they returned. Three days passed, he says, before they returned. Ichazo's body was so rigid he had to be lifted off the post. Back in his hut, his personality structure broke down completely, after which he was transformed. When he went to the apartment, he found the men waiting for him. Now, they said, he could join the group.

According to whichever account may be true, either one or four years later he returned to La Paz. There, he either discovered, or created, the system of the enneagramatic psychological fixations. The versions, or amplifications, of what happened differ in part. In the earliest he said he received or discovered the knowledge from the 'Green Qu Tub' or the Archangel Gabriel. More recently, that he created the application but was "in a state of 'divine presence.' Metatron is the prince of archangels and an archetypal figure for the concentration of the relative mind, you know. At this point, I started visualizing the Enneagons in front of me. They didn't just appear. I started visualizing it. It was not that some Archangel Metatron came and said, 'Here it is.' If things were that simple and ridiculous—my God."

Thereafter, in 1951 or 1955, Ichazo began teaching groups. He also made trips to Nepal, Kashmir, the Hindu Kush and Afghanistan. Originally, he said he made contact with the same school from which Gurdjieff came. Ichazo says he was given much knowledge during his journeys, allowed to read the Akashic records, and at the death of one of the five elders of what he will only call "the School," he became the Qu Tub, or center, the one who was to carry the knowledge to the West.

On October 1, 1969, in Santiago, Chile, Oscar Ichazo gave a series of lectures at the *Instituto de Psicologia Aplicada* on the enneagram as a means of mapping the human psyche and its character fixations. Among the attendees was Dr. Claudio B. Naranjo, an expert on various psychotropic substances and a research associate at the University of Chile who had introduced feeling-and image-enhancing drugs to psychotherapy. Naranjo had studied at Harvard on a Fulbright Scholarship and was now a Guggenheim Fellow at the University of California at Berkeley. While at Berkeley, he had received letters from fellow psychoanalysts and a former patient extolling Ichazo's esoteric knowledge, particularly of Naranjo's specialty, human typology. Although unimpressed with Ichazo himself—"His total impact on me as a person did not impress me in any way"—Naranjo found himself "awed by the completeness of his theoretical picture and techniques."

Naranjo spent two months with Ichazo and a group of twenty-seven Chileans with whom he worked. He then returned to California. Naranjo had extensive connections with Esalen, then the center of the human potential movement, and with Berkeley's psychological community, particularly the Center for Biochemical Dynamics (where he had continued his study of typology and the effects of hallucinogenic drugs, such as LSD, psylocybin, mescaline and *yajé*, a shamanic drug growing in the jungles of the Colombian Andes, the same drug taken by Ichazo).

Naranjo spoke informally to a good many of his friends about his experiences with Ichazo, who in the meantime asked Naranjo to see if Americans would be interested in working with him in a ten-month program. That May, in 1970, Naranjo gave a talk at Esalen telling of his experience with Ichazo, saying he "claimed to be somebody who had been schooled or 'accepted' in the same Sufi tradition that was the source of Gurdjieff's training." Ichazo, he said, was explicit about differentiating "'the School' from traditional Sufi orders, including the Naqshbandi." According to Ichazo, while some Sufi orders derived from the School, it was not Sufi. About his personal impression of Ichazo, Naranjo said that although he seemed to have "an authoritarian streak that I don't trust" and that "I don't like him as a person," he found that "his bag of tricks is incredible." Soon, all the talk in spiritual and psychological circles at Esalen and Berkeley was about Ichazo.

Hearing about Ichazo from Naranjo, the scientist John Lilly decided to spend a week with him and flew down to Arica, Chile, a rapidly growing fishing port of 100,000 people, most living in old packing crates, near the Peruvian border. It was a desert and, according to Lilly, "one of the driest places on earth." Ichazo's school, he said, was called the *Instituto de Gnosologia* and was "billed as a center for the revival of an ancient esoteric school of mysticism." He found a balding man of medium height with prominent, dark brown eyes. Though his physical appearance did not live up to "the visual expectation of a 'holy man,'" Lilly was impressed, like Naranjo, with Ichazo's knowledge. Unlike Naranjo, he found Ichazo a

"warm, likable human being who was practical, prag-
matic, direct and had boundless energy. He is very positive and never criticizes third parties."

When the ten-month course began on July 1, 1970,
fifty-four Americans, Naranjo and Lilly among them,
were in attendance. The days were long, fifteen and more
hours filled with gymnastics, meditation, talks and
experiments. During the training, Naranjo is said to have
gone into a satori state and refused to return. Ichazo had
to bring him back. Angry, Naranjo returned. Things
apparently went wrong with Naranjo after that, for after
seven months he was expelled by the group as undesirable. According to Ichazo, "Naranjo was rejected by
100% of the vote [of the group]. The main reason being
that he could not drop his 'messianic' attitude that was
felt as very individualistic and egocentric." Lilly stayed
on and had many conversations with Ichazo, among
them a talk about divine grace in which Ichazo used the
Sufi term for it, *baraka*. Then they discussed the training:

> *Lilly:* What sort of name are you giving it? Is this the Sufi
> thing or is this something else?
> *Ichazo:* We call it always "The School."
> *Lilly:* People want a label. The Sufi name in the United
> States has a lot of prestige....
> *Ichazo:* It is better for us, John, that the name is something new
> because the teaching is completely new. If we confuse our
> names, for instance with Sufism, everybody is going prepared
> for that way. Let us make it something new.

Lilly left Arica before he completed the program. He
gives differing accounts of when he left, saying after six
months, later eight. He left then either a month before or
after Naranjo. A lot of reasons are given, but it seems
clear that he wanted to maintain what he considered his
independence as a "scientific explorer." He said, "I did
not like the idea of being in a closed group, esoteric or

otherwise. I have pursued my own path, learning from whomever and wherever I could...."

Returning to Berkeley, Claudio Naranjo focused his entire energies on understanding the enneagram material that Ichazo had presented. Naranjo had first learned of the enneagram in his teens when reading Ouspensky's *Search*. It is not clear but he may have joined a Gurdjieff group in Venezuela, leaving after a short time. Having a negative attitude toward the existing Gurdjieff teaching represented by Lord Pentland—"I had been disappointed in the extent to which Gurdjieff's school entailed a living lineage," he says—Naranjo had to rely on his own research abetted by the likely use of feeling and imagery enhancers.

Intently studying all the publicly available Gurdjieff literature and Ichazo's enneagram material of psychological compulsions, Naranjo saw a correspondence between what Ichazo was saying and Christianity's seven deadly sins. He then related this, along with information on the zodiac, to the various psychological typologies (histrionic, compulsive, avoidant or schizoid, and so forth) elaborated in *The Diagnostic and Statistical Manual of Mental Disorders* (DSM) and soon developed, as he would say, his own enneagrammatic "collage." However, he was "under a commitment of reserve" to Oscar Ichazo in regard to teaching the personality enneagram. So Naranjo wrote to Ichazo asking for permission to teach. Ichazo never answered. "I took the fact that he didn't reply," said Naranjo, "as a sign that I myself had to decide."

In 1971 he formed his own school and called it SAT (Seekers After Truth). This was a particularly fertile time to start an 'esoteric school.' Having sought the spiritual with drugs—"LSD is America's Jesus Christ," said the Indian holy man Meher Baba—many young people were looking for a way to get high without them. With his extensive knowledge of drugs, human typology, and now a version of the enneagram, Naranjo's school soon had upwards of a hundred students.

Oscar Ichazo, perhaps sensing the propitiousness of the time, came to America, also in 1971, and started his own school. Readers of the September 24 edition of the *New York Times* were greeted with a full-page advertisement showing the enneagram and announcing a three-month Arica Training program. Price: $3,000 with *satori* a guarantee. The advertisement was misleading in that satori, a Zen Buddhist word, meant for Ichazo not a state of intuitive illumination, but a heightened sense of well-being and happiness. Nevertheless, the course enrolled seventy-six students. At its end Ichazo announced, "I am the roots of a new tradition" and urged everyone to work very hard "for if mankind refuses to seek enlightenment, then, within the next ten years there will be a holocaust which can and probably will destroy the planet."

During the training program, John Lilly showed up but was refused admission. He had written a book, *The Center of the Cyclone*, and gave Ichazo the manuscript. It was a description of his LSD experiences, together with a lengthy section on his experiences in Arica. He was told if he would not publish it he could join the training. Lilly refused and his relationship with Ichazo ended. But his book—full of the colorful inner adventures he had, supposedly as a result of practicing Arica Training—gave Arica a big boost. (It would take eighteen years for Lilly to admit that "in fact, LSD was the key ingredient" in his experiences. He said that while at Arica, he had "dosed himself with LSD about every four weeks.")

As months and years went on, the media carried many articles about Arica. Though Ichazo characterized the Arica Training as a new teaching, its obvious correspondence on many counts with Gurdjieff's Fourth Way soon became a sticking point. How could his Arica teaching be new when so many things were clearly borrowed? Initially, Ichazo ignored the comparison, but as the years passed became increasingly negative, vehemently attacking both Gurdjieff and his teaching. Eventually, he withdrew to Maui leaving the lower levels of the Arica teaching to others.

IN BERKELEY, MEANWHILE, NARANJO TAUGHT HIS VERSION of the personality enneagram to two groups. In the first were members of SAT who at Naranjo's insistence signed a commitment that "nobody was to teach this." The second group, unaffiliated with SAT, was more informal. Lectures and demonstrations were given during nine or ten evenings over a period of months and no one was asked to sign a secrecy agreement. (This was the group to which Helen Palmer belonged.) He didn't demand a commitment of secrecy, Naranjo said, because after so short a time he "didn't foresee that anybody would venture to teach the characterology."

Earlier Naranjo had met Kathleen Riordan Speeth. As her parents had studied with Orage and Gurdjieff, Speeth had literally grown up in the Work. She was acquainted with everyone, had access to a great deal of information, and had practiced the movements from an early age. After receiving a doctorate in B. F. Skinner-derived behavioral psychology from Columbia University in New York in 1967, she moved to San Francisco and became a member of the Gurdjieff Foundation and a pupil of Lord John Pentland. A friend of Pamela Travers, the creator of Mary Poppins and a long-time Gurdjieffian, Speeth accompanied Travers to a talk in Berkeley. There she met Naranjo who told her of his own school and his "Fourth Way background." Fascinated with his "collage" of the deadly sins and DSM categories as applied to the enneagram, Speeth talked with Naranjo many times, eventually becoming romantically involved. She soon left the Foundation for

SAT. With her intimate knowledge of the Gurdjieff Work, at least at the exoteric level, Speeth was quite a catch for Naranjo. He soon made her a group leader and had her teach the Gurdjieff movements, which, up to that time had stayed within the teaching.

By 1975 SAT began to falter. Primary among the reasons were Naranjo's drug use and the acrimony among its members in either defending their personality fixations or attacking others for theirs. Hearing of a Gurdjieff teacher in New York, Naranjo flew there and invited him to speak in Berkeley to SAT "graduates" who were dissatisfied and at loose ends. The New York teacher had himself only begun teaching a few years previously and had no experience with the main line of Gurdjieff work. His first teacher was the faux-Gurdjieffian Alex Horn who had passed him on to David Daniels who claimed to have spent some time at Mendham, New Jersey (Ouspensky's estate). When Daniels suffered a nervous breakdown, his group fell apart and he moved to Cambridge. Three years later, the New York teacher, having re-established contact with Daniels, began to commute to Berkeley to teach Naranjo's pupils, among them the Kuwaiti psychologist A. H. Almaas who, saying he was "fulfilled," later set himself up as a teacher and created "The Diamond Approach," a synthesis of psychology, Sufism and an *ersatz* Gurdjieff. Naranjo, having divested himself of responsibility for SAT, returned to South America.

Kathleen Speeth, following Naranjo's departure, taught the personality enneagram to Helen Palmer and many others, regularly giving seminars until the mid-1980s. Palmer subsequently set up her own 'school' and began teaching the enneagram typology. Declared Naranjo from Spain where he now resides, "I am sure that not even Helen Palmer would have done so without tutoring from one of those early students of mine who succumbed to the temptation to teach." Speeth continued to teach in Berkeley until the late 1980s although she had moved to East Hampton, New York, having been taken up into the fear of the day that a tidal wave was going to engulf the Bay Area. At no time did she or Palmer require their students to sign a secrecy agreement.

Speeth, in time, began to see "the potential for harm" in teaching the enneagram personality fixations. Despite good intentions, people's shadow side would use it in destructive ways. "I can no longer take the karmic burden of passing this on," she said and promised to stop teaching. "There's a lot of reasons to teach it," she said. "There is a lot of money to be made, a lot of prestige to be had, but it cannot be used for transcendence. Truly, I must say I have never seen anyone develop using the enneagram of personality."

Meanwhile, Father Robert Ochs, who along with Helen Palmer had taken the nine or so evening teachings of the enneagram from Naranjo, had returned to Loyola University in Chicago where he created the first college level course in the enneagram. Father Ochs adapted Naranjo's typology to correspond to Catholicism's seven capital sins—anger, pride, envy, avarice, gluttony, lust, and sloth. Again, of course, with the admonishment that all that was learned was to be kept secret. Said Father Pat O'Leary, also a Jesuit: "There was a great emphasis on secrecy—and a total violation of same. Bob taught that we were not to pass it on. And here he was passing it on. And, of course, we glibly talked about it to anyone who'd listen." Father O'Leary soon took the enneagram public by co-authoring the first book on the subject. This was followed with books by Don Riso, an ex-Jesuit, Helen Palmer and later Naranjo, as well as their students, and the students of their students. With that, the enneagram genie was out of the bottle and into the marketplace.

In 1989 Ichazo's Arica Institute, claiming copyright infringement, sued Father O'Leary and other priests and nuns who had written about the enneagram. Said Ichazo: "What they have done is just a brutal and massive misappropriation, and with the worst of manners. They say they have discovered some old Sufi tradition. What the hell do they mean by this, I would like to know. The entire theory originated in me exclusively....What I want is a full explanation with public acknowledgment." The suit was settled out of court with a signed statement to that effect.

Two years later Ichazo had Arica sue Palmer for copyright infringement. His lawyers argued that Palmer's teaching of the enneagram was theoretically wrong, that she departed from the accepted dogma and had divorced the enneagram from its spiritual and philosophical moorings. Arica held that Ichazo had discovered the fixations and that they were objective scientific fact. The court held that if this was so, then Arica could have no legal claim to ownership and saw its lawsuit as "an effort to prevent heresy" and refused to involve itself, contending that Palmer had a right to teach, wrongly or rightly, what she wanted. On appeal to the Second U.S. Circuit Court, Arica claimed that Ichazo had not discovered but rather created the enneagrammatic fixation system. The court saw this as "an inconsistent claim (to what Arica had previously said about 'discovery') so as to better serve its position in litigation." The court ruled that "Ichazo's attachment of labels to the enneagram figure contains the minimal degree of creativity necessary to make it copyrightable." However, the court ruled Palmer's use of the enneagram was "fair use" and she could continue to teach—as she subsequently has.

The road to legitimacy was further paved in August 1994 when Palmer and a number of other enneagrammers combined efforts to stage the First International

Enneagram Conference at prestigious Stanford University. Notably missing were Oscar Ichazo and Claudio Naranjo, although the three-day conference was dedicated to them (as well as G. I. Gurdjieff). Ichazo remained incommunicado, but Naranjo did send several representatives and made a video for the occasion. In his long, rather rambling talk, Naranjo said that Ichazo "didn't talk about the enneagrams of personality more than two hours during our year with him." When he taught in Berkeley, Naranjo said, "I was not 'doing Arica,' was not echoing what had been Oscar's offer to us. I was working in my own way, putting out my own collage, so to say." Further: "I was not happy with the fact that the commitment to secrecy was not kept, that the enneagram came to the streets a little prematurely. I felt critical of people taking initiative in writing about information that had not been originated by them, and who were acquainted with only a fragment of a traditional body of knowledge that is considerably more complex."

In a *Gnosis* magazine interview in 1996, Naranjo is even more explicit, calling the enneagram movement his "bastard child" and speaking about "the shallowness, bad taste, and general immaturity reflected in the current enneagram books and magazines." But what caused the ensuing uproar was his contention that "It seems to me the questionable ethics of the earliest teachers has had cultural consequences, for I see the movement as pervaded by a combination of greed and arrogance and by a great disrespect toward the sources of the knowledge, to the extent of insinuating that the tradition is a myth."

A year later Palmer hit back in an interview in the same magazine declaring that "Ichazo booted Naranjo out of the 1970 Arica training, castigating him for selling out the mystical tradition to greedy psychologists. Now Naranjo does what was done to himself—castigating and trying to erase the transformative spiritual work developing in the next generation." Further: "I don't like a lot of what's happening in the [enneagram] community either—and it's terrible to be a focus of hatred, because I see the enneagram bridging both worldly and esoteric interests."

Naranjo's letter of response was short. "I don't delight in hurting people, and I am sorry that sometimes the truth is uncomfortable. I am also sincerely sorry to think that the bad karma of some enneagram plunderers (who have tried to make me look small to look taller themselves) has polluted the enneagram community, making it perhaps more resistant to transformative influences. Yet I have said what I have said...."

LEAVING OSCAR ICHAZO ASIDE FOR THE MOMENT, IT IS interesting to recapitulate the principles—or lack thereof—by which the personality enneagram came to market. It begins with Naranjo, thrown out of Arica for a "messianic attitude." This judgment by his peers and his teacher apparently makes little impression on him for he then asks his teacher for permission to teach, receives silence in reply, takes that as a license, and opens up a 'school.' He takes the name SAT, Seekers After Truth, the name of the society Gurdjieff and his fellow seekers established in 1895. Naranjo's only connection with Gurdjieff, or the ancient teaching of the Fourth Way which he brought, is through his meager seven months of study with Ichazo. That he believes himself thereby qualified to set up a 'school,' appropriate a Fourth Way term for its name, and teach, among other things, the enneagram, shows a mentality that is unfortunately all too contemporary. Naranjo, a psychoanalyst whose speciality was and is character and personality, believing that his students would, or could, keep a secrecy agreement is, to say the least, amazingly incredulous.

Speaking of this time, Naranjo recalled, "The situation was very different from Arica. It was not individuals 'working-on-self' according to theory. It was rather a group in which there was room for therapeutic interaction and group-dynamics which I interpreted and confronted." In other words, it was an encounter group in which Naranjo was the authority; a position, or fixation, from which he has never deviated. From this group work, Naranjo claimed that he, and not Ichazo, produced "in light of passions and fixations originated [within the group] the descriptions of character types that now have become well known." (Later, Ichazo was to publish his own interpretation.)

But was the personality enneagram an original creation of Naranjo's? Or did he—having been first acquainted with the idea by Ichazo, who in turn had likely been introduced to it by the Fourth Way group in Buenos Aires—get the idea from the Fourth Way books of C. S. Nott, Fritz Peters, and Ouspensky? In 1969, C. S. Nott, one of Gurdjieff's earliest and closest English students, published a book, *Journey Through This World*. Speaking about chief feature, Nott wrote that "in each one of us is a key to our actions and manifestations. It tips the scales....It is something mechanical and imaginary...and *it arises from one or more of the seven deadly sins*, but chiefly from self-love and vanity. One can discover it by becoming more conscious; and its discovery brings an increase of consciousness." [Emphasis added.] Much has been made of Naranjo's applying the seven deadly sins to the enneagram, some even seeing it as a mark of "genius." But was it? Or did Naranjo, a voracious reader of the esoteric and all books Gurdjieffian, more likely read about it in Nott's book?

Naranjo certainly would have read Fritz Peters' book *Gurdjieff Remembered*, published in 1971, the same year Naranjo was expelled from Arica and returned to Berkeley. In it, Peters relates a long conversation with Gurdjieff about astrological signs. The signs, Gurdjieff said, "were originally 'invented' to synthesize the particular characteristics against which a given individual would have to fight—or to struggle—in the course of his life on earth....Gurdjieff did not discuss all the signs in detail, but suggested that once one could discover, *for oneself,* what the sign symbolized or represented in the way of characteristics (or compulsions) in one's self, then one would have to remind oneself that such a synthesis represented those elements against which one would have to fight throughout life—what might be called the 'built-in obstacles' in one's own nature that were part of the key to 'self-perfection' or growth; the *necessary* obstacles standing in the path to development. He added that, as was usual in all great, ancient sciences, the lesson was never clearly stated, but could only be learned with effort..." Certainly Naranjo, with his long training and interest in human typology, would have understood the many ramifications of seeing one's characteristics as compulsions, and of the astrological signs portraying those characteristics as necessary obstacles to be struggled against, not accepted. And so two books within a year of each other gave Naranjo, a specialist in typology, the keys to the "enneagram kingdom" that others not having his interest or training would not put together.

Collecting and then cross-referencing all the information that Nott and Peters gave, along with what Ouspensky provided in *Search* about types and the enneagram (too long to be quoted), Naranjo could simply fit the pieces together to form what might be called the exoteric version of enneagram typology. Like Ichazo before him, Naranjo was a good detective. However, that the real and ancient formulation of types to which Gurdjieff alluded—and purposely did not make public—might exist at the esoteric level of the teaching he brought never seems to have occurred to Naranjo, or to Ichazo, Palmer, and their followers.

Further, as Gurdjieff made clear, the student is, through long and keen observation of his recurring individual manifestation, to come to his chief weakness/psychological fixation himself. Then when the student's observations are affirmed, the depth of recognition strikes a lasting imprint throughout the whole of his being. By contrast, when one is told their personality fixation, it is akin to taking a drug. They have not worked and purified themselves but passively accept what they are told. And, of course, this contemporary version may not be entirely correct.

Naranjo has also been credited with creating the idea of panels of specific types, which was to become a cornerstone of subsequent enneagram teaching. But a careful reading of *Search* shows the idea's true origin. Ouspensky reported Gurdjieff as saying: "Each of you has probably met in life people of one and the same type. Such people often even look like one another, and their inner reactions to things are exactly the same. What one likes the other will like. What one does not like the other will not like. You must remember such occasions because you can study the science of types only by meeting types."

That Naranjo now takes the high road for himself, speaking of others as "plunderers" with "greed and arrogance and a great disrespect" toward the sources of the knowledge and tradition, is simply to excuse, in his terms, "the bastard child" he fathered. And he still attaches himself to the Fourth Way. In his latest book on the enneagram, for example, he speaks of his view as a "Fourth Way view" and takes a number of Fourth Way ideas and renders them in psychoanalytic language. He also is a proponent of what he calls the "self-diagnostic process"— that one can free oneself from his chief weakness simply by being told about it.

Naranjo has never accepted the primary tenet of the Fourth Way—that man is a machine who is asleep to himself and therefore cannot wake up to himself without a teacher. There has always been a struggle between spiritual and secular, sacred and profane. In our time it is seen in the theft of the spiritual which is then watered down into secular psychology and abused by the therapist-who-would-be-priest. Lastly, and most seriously, injecting esoteric ideas and practices into society weakens and distorts not only the teachings from which they are stolen, but corrupts society itself. For these ideas and practices are powerful in themselves, and when introduced into secular life they will necessarily be taken over by the ego and used for its own glorification and the domination of others.

AS THERE ARE ELEMENTS OF CONTRITION IN NARANJO'S public statements, not so with his disowned protégé Helen Palmer who still regularly traces her 'lineage' to Naranjo. Wrote Clarence Thomson, editor of the *Enneagram Educator:* "When Helen Palmer talks about an oral tradition, she makes it plain on a number of occasions that the oral tradition to which she belongs has its origins in Claudio Naranjo's living room." Disowned or not Palmer, a self-proclaimed counter phobic point six on the enneagram personality scale, carries the enneagram torch far and wide—"I've gotten into hyperdrive about the enneagram," she declared.

In opposition to what all traditional teachings hold, Palmer believes that esoteric knowledge can be thrown into ordinary life and somehow awaken people who are otherwise unprepared. She speaks of "the oral tradition" of the enneagram which, in her case, must move from Ichazo to Naranjo to herself, overlooking the open and continued rejection of Naranjo by Ichazo. Since Palmer only studied with Naranjo for nine evenings, in terms of time alone this 'oral tradition' is certainly unique. Anyone familiar with the term oral tradition knows that her use is as self-serving as it is inauthentic. It is the same with spiritual practices and exercises which she chooses to call 'technologies' (no doubt taken from Werner Erhard's Est, another instance of contemporary plundering of the spiritual).

By thus neutering the teaching, severing it from its original spiritual basis, she can build her own 'psychotechnology.' She writes, "I am committed to drawing upon the best possible intuitive technology for different types of people, regardless of the system that produces it." She also has little regard for those who strive to maintain the purity of their teaching—"There is an arrogance, a snootiness, a bizarre kind of self-referencing, that is largely unrecognized among many highly developed spiritual practitioners. It bugs me." Instead of attempting to understand their point of view, she psychologizes them—"However developed they may be at their particular small tour de force in the entire spectrum of consciousness, they really need to keep this private for their own psychological benefit. It's for their own comfort and sense of speciality, not necessarily for the good of all."

Palmer, a former left-wing activist, seems to frame life through the lenses of a contemporary secular humanist psychologist, one who believes that by bringing the spiritual down to ground level everyone will benefit. She doesn't understand that, as Gurdjieff often said, people are asleep, they are machines, they have no indivisible I, they exist almost completely in the chains of their egoism. She certainly is not an esotericist—"Gurdjieff was a contemporary of Freud's; there was no psychology then....I hardly think he could have had any possibility of organizing the material in the way that is now possible in our generation, with all of its public availability of psychological understanding. There was no psychology at that time...."

IF PALMER WRITES GURDJIEFF OFF AS NOT BEING PSYCHOLOGICALLY sophisticated, Oscar Ichazo, though once having claimed

41

he was "Gurdjieff's pupil," completely savages him in the 1991 "The Teachings of The Great Telesmatta" issue of *The Arican.* (His teaching is filled with words like *Divine Metatelos, Telegnostic Meditations, Trialectics, Toham Kum Rah,* and the like.) In a sometimes ranting and elliptical prose, fuming over being referred to by enneagrammers as "a mystical 'fruitcake' who has visions," and his teaching being labeled by the media as a Gurdjieff-derivative, Ichazo's long essay completely disowns any Gurdjieffian influence.

He begins by claiming none of Gurdjieff's ideas are new: "I would like to say very clearly that there is not one single original 'idea' of any importance in the entire work of Mr. Gurdjieff....I read *All and Everything* and I found that Mr. Gurdjieff was, in fact, not only mediocre but a very bad writer with no idea of composition or how to develop and present his themes." He castigates Gurdjieff's cosmology as a "very old and naive materialistic cosmology." It would be beyond the sphere of the present inquiry to go into this more deeply, except to point out that ten years earlier in a 1981 interview, "I Am The Root of a New Tradition," Ichazo enunciated a different view. "In the spiritual area, the last area we are going to know because it is the highest, we are going to reach the point where the spirit has limits, *where the spirit is material. It's a different type of matter, but material anyhow."* [Emphasis added.] For the careful reader, Gurdjieff's usage of materiality has many levels of meaning. Regarding the age of the teaching he brought, as previously mentioned, Gurdjieff said it was very old, independent of other lines, and hitherto unknown. He also said, speaking of Christianity, "People have forgotten that it is a school" and that the Christian church and form of worship were "all taken in a ready-made form from Egypt, only not from the Egypt that we know but from one which we do not know....Prehistoric Egypt was Christian many thousands of years before the birth of Christ....Special schools existed in this prehistoric Egypt." According to Gurdjieff, then, the ancient teaching he brought, reformulated for our time, had its origin in prehistoric Egypt.

With this in mind we can now recognize the misperception in Ichazo's contentions about Gurdjieff's teaching. Ichazo believes he traces the ideas through Pythagoras, Middle Platonism, Stoics, Epicureans, Gnostics, Pseudo-Dionysius, and finally the Catholic Church. He makes the common mistake of assuming that because the Fourth Way did not appear in the West until 1912, older teachings predate it and are its source. But as Gurdjieff said of the teaching: It has been completely unknown up to the present time. Thus, a complete revolution of our contemporary mentality is required if we are to consider seriously that the Fourth Way in reality may predate our historical Egyptian-Judaic-Christian heritage.

Not having studied Ichazo's teaching, one is not in a position to evaluate its worth, but some of its history can be examined. Although completely disowning any debt to Gurdjieff, he admits to first learning about the enneagram in Ouspensky's *Search*. Later he joins a group in Buenos Aires—"being its guinea pig," he said at one time—that may have been a Fourth Way group or at least one greatly influenced by its teaching. He makes no mention of what he learned there, but chief feature had been known orally for some time to those associated with the Fourth Way teaching. C. S. Nott would later publish some hint of it in his book *Journey Through This World*. Besides alluding to the seven deadly sins and chief feature, he wrote: "On types: If you observe yourself and note the things that attract you, what you like to see, to hear, to taste, touch, you may discover your type. Types begin with 3—man number 1, 2, 3; physical, emotional, mental. The blending of these in different proportions determines the twelve basic types; then the division into twenty-seven; and subdivision into seventy-two types." Also, there is Rodney Collin's book, *Theory of Celestial Influence*, published in 1954 at about the same time that Ichazo began teaching. Collin, a pupil of Ouspensky's, speaks of the glands and six human types—Lunar, Mercurial, Venusian, Martial, Jovial and Saturnine—and sets the types around an enneagram and speaks of the "inner circulation" taking place between these types.

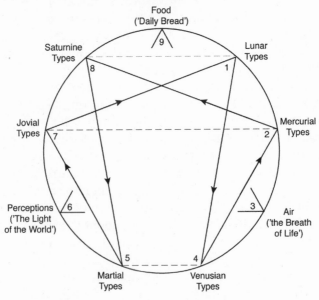

The Types of Humanity—Rodney Collin

Armed with these esoteric ideas or even perhaps with a system of typology he received from the Buenos Aires group, Ichazo was in a position to construct his elaborate psychological theory of the deadly sins based on the enneagram. So the particular vehemence with which he tries to discredit Gurdjieff may have its root not in a new tradition but in the very debt that he owes and denies. Interestingly, the lack of acknowledgment of one's teacher is a spiritual symptom peculiar to our time.

From the first, Ichazo said he wanted to make the Arica system public, which is why he gave the series of talks in 1969 in Santiago to psychologists. That these psychologists would use this material in support of their own views and research, as Naranjo did, does not seem to have occurred to him. With Naranjo's help, Ichazo then formed a secret mystical society, which would seem contradictory to his stated intention of openness. Afterwards, he came to New York City, ran a full page advertisement in the *New York Times* using the enneagram symbol and announced the Arica training. "Never before has it been possible almost to engineer your own path," he declared." This word 'engineer' might be repulsive to someone who is mystical, because in mysticism things which go along with reason are not only unacceptable, but seem contradictory. That is because *until now there was no logic that could grasp unity, and so reason has been thought to be opposed to the spiritual path.*" [Emphasis added.]

As he clearly has studied Gurdjieff's Fourth Way, and without attribution incorporated many of its principles, his statement is peculiar since the cornerstone of the Fourth Way is objective reason, conscience and the unity of knowledge. As Gurdjieff stated, "One of the most central of the ideas of objective knowledge is the idea of the unity of everything, of unity in diversity."

Within five years or so, Ichazo retreated to a walled compound on Maui saying that "The teacher comes in, more or less, in the eighth or ninth level of the School." One would have to be a member of his school to know what is going on, but whatever Ichazo's "engineering," no student could be qualified to teach after only five years. Identification with sleep, false personality, imagination and buffers are simply too strong.

As a result, after an initial fast start, Arica's membership appears to have stabilized and, other than the enneagram fireworks with Naranjo and Palmer, Arica and Oscar Ichazo are little heard from. From time to time he has said "I will be publishing the entire theory in the near future," so that may or may not be in the offing. In retrospect it seems as though he made some initial strategic errors that quickly cut the force of his teaching. For all his psychological acumen, he completely misread Naranjo and Lilly. They had a long and well-known history of drug taking with all the false individualism and fantasy, personal and collective, which this entails. As their experiences were not the result of long, disciplined spiritual work on false personality, but instead drug induced, there was no ego-reduction but only a grandiosity masked with an intellectual's supposed objectivity.

The main tenet of all true teachings is that man is asleep, engulfed in dreams and ego. He cannot help but use everything wrongly in order to maintain his vaunted 'individuality.' Why did Ichazo think he could introduce into the mainstream of ego life, with little to no preparation, a powerful esoteric tool like the enneagram and not have it totally distorted? Δ

Part II

People of the Bookmark

The Fellowship of Friends is an organization for spiritual development which purports to base itself on the Fourth Way. Founded by Robert Earl Burton, the Fellowship caught the crest of a strong wave of spirituality that swept America in the 1970s and was soon able to establish its Gurdjieff-Ouspensky Centres in many of the major cities of America and Europe. It has recently opened centers in Russia, South America and some parts of Asia. The Fellowship is headquartered in rural Northern California where it has created a small community with its own school, museum, theater and arts groups, as well as a winery. While membership has declined in recent years because of scandals and lawsuits involving its founder, there are still said to be some two thousand members worldwide, all of whom are expected to tithe ten percent of their income, as well as make extra donations for the founder's birthday and *special projects. The Fellowship, which has legal status as a church, has an annual income of some $5 million. Its founder is reported to receive an annual salary of $250,000.*

T ALL, ENERGETIC, AND AMBITIOUS, WITH AN APPEAL-ING UTOPIAN VISION, ROBERT EARL BURTON, THE former fourth grade school teacher from North Little Rock, Arkansas, founded The Fellowship of Friends in 1970, and soon proved himself a master of New Age positioning and promotion. Promising prospective students both immortality and the creation of an "Ark" that would protect them from the coming Armageddon which he prophesied, Burton gratified the idealistic and naive mentality of the times. Taking the idea for his Ark from Warren M. Miller Jr.'s popular science fiction novel of the day, *A Canticle for Leibowitz*, in which monks of the Order of St. Leibowitz preserved ancient knowledge in a monastery while the world underwent a modern Dark Age, Burton soon had enough students to purchase 365 acres of property in rural Northern California which he named Renaissance, now renamed Apollo. Here Burton built his Ark. His students cleared and terraced the rolling hills for a vineyard and built a commercial winery, planted sprawling rose gardens, dug a man-made lake, and built a theater and a private museum featuring a collection of 17th century Chinese furniture (recently auctioned at Christie's for $11.2 million), and for Burton a French chateau filled with costly paintings, marble busts of Homer and Milton, Aubusson carpets, and ornately inlaid turn-of-the-century Steinway grand pianos, and Sevres china.

As he reshaped his acreage, Burton refocused the Fourth Way teaching, retaining Gurdjieff's name because of its drawing power, but reorienting and repackaging it. The Burton-ized Fourth Way based itself not on Gurdjieff's intentionally enigmatic and negative presentation but on that of his student, the more accessible Ouspensky (with a smattering of ideas of his student, Rodney Collin). But the real key to the success of Burton's Fellowship of Friends was his breaking of a major tenet of the Fourth Way teaching, the idea that the prospective student had to *find* the teaching. The teaching was not to be advertised or in any way overtly promoted. Burton changed all that. He printed thousands upon thousands of slick oversized four-color bookmarks, each displaying romantically painted busts of Gurdjieff and Ouspensky, along with phone numbers of his Gurdjieff-Ouspensky Centres. Students were instructed to regularly canvas bookstores and libraries and slip the bookmarks into any book that spoke of the Fourth Way teaching—hence the name "the Bookmark People." For the unsuspecting reader, the logical assumption, of course, was that there was a connection between the bookmark and the books in which they were found. With this cunning deceit, some eight thousand seekers "found" the teaching by dialing the advertised telephone number.

Though Burton claimed to be a Fourth Way teacher, he himself never had an authentic Fourth Way teacher. The level of his understanding of the teaching was based on what he could pick up from Fourth Way books and from his one-time teacher, the actor-director Alexander Francis Horn. Horn, himself a faux-Gurdjieffian without any real connection to the Fourth Way, had based his own understanding on books and on that of his first wife Carol, a student of John Bennett's ten-month experimental program—an eclectic melding of the Fourth Way with other teachings and practices. Horn first taught in New York and later in San Francisco where he created the Theatre of All Possibilities, a theater which purported to double as a Fourth Way school. Horn financially exploited his students, manipulated their lives, often physically brutalizing them—all in the name of the teaching.

The thirty-one-year-old Burton, dismissed by Horn after a year or so for not "staying on task," apparently picked up enough from Horn to start his own teaching. Proclaiming that he had attained the level of understanding of a man number five, a high degree of unity, Burton began to gather students. What he actually understood of the teaching has always been in question. This had been difficult to determine since he was reclusive, giving no public talks and publishing no books. However, this changed with the publication of his book, *Self-Remembering*.

BURTON DEVOTES AN ENTIRE BOOK TO A SUBJECT WHICH Gurdjieff, in his published writings, rarely refers to—it is mentioned only twice in his *First Series*, for example—and is given only a preliminary explanation in Ouspensky's *In Search of the Miraculous*. Given the decisiveness of Burton's title—*Self-Remembering*—and its 216-page length, a reader might be justified in expecting a detailed and knowledgeable exploration of the special state of self-remembering. Strangely, that is lacking.

Burton begins by describing self-remembering as "your dormant self is remembering to be awake." Although the formulation sounds good, its usefulness is limited-to-nil since Burton does not say what he means by the key terms *self* and *awake*. Later, he will say, "It's not easy to discuss self-remembering because, in its highest form, it is a non-verbal process." Of course, in their highest forms all spiritual practices are non-verbal, but as lower forms can be delineated and discussed, it's not clear why Burton isn't more helpful.

Now and then concrete statements are put forward, and this *is* helpful, although perhaps not as Burton imagines. "Generally, self-remembering must originate in the intellectual part of the emotional center," he says, "because remembering oneself is an emotional experience." Logically, this is consistent, but is it true? As Ouspensky says, emotions do need to be involved to reach higher levels of self-remembering, but the self-remembering needn't originate in the emotional center. For beginners in particular, it first originates in the intellectual part of the intellectual center.

A whole chapter is devoted to divided attention. Here Burton says: "Divided attention is self-remembering: they are synonymous. The state of divided attention encompasses a wide spectrum of emotions." While the division of one's attention is important, it is simply the first of many actions that the process within the state of self-remembering requires. Burton's formulation, as far as it goes, is only preliminary. It's somewhat akin to saying that to drive a car you put a key in the ignition.

About the division of attention itself, only the vaguest, most generalized instruction is given and the explanation, unfortunately, is circular. "When you are in essence," advises Burton, "you try to divide attention. Try to look at these flowers and, at the same time, be aware that you are looking at them. Dividing attention puts one in essence." This raises a number of questions: Must we be in essence to divide attention? Or does dividing attention put us in essence? How does one come into essence? How does one know it is essence? Gurdjieff quite flatly said the work must begin from personality. We cannot work from essence until we have worked through personality.

As to what attention is divided between, Burton makes only one comment: "Self remembering means that one is aware both of oneself and of what one is viewing. If one views an object without being aware of oneself…" Is the "one" which Burton speaks of as being aware what he takes to be the real, or permanent I? Interestingly, if one has a strong mind and ego-will, one can resolutely keep the mind relatively clear, and so, self-locked in the mind, suppose *that* is the real I of which Gurdjieff speaks, when in fact one's center of gravity is still located in the head.

There is a tendency for pupils to make the act of observing, or the awareness, into an observer, an entity, thus maintaining the self-image, which then is reinterpreted as the "spiritual I." This reification of observing into an observer-entity was Gurdjieff's criticism of Orage. One wonders if Burton has fallen into the same trap and, not having a teacher to point out this fundamental error, has unwittingly guided himself (and thereby his students) into a spiritual backwater. The question occurs too as to why Burton does not speak of "I's", other than making a few references? This is a major psychological tenet of the teaching.

Burton appears to be very much interested in control and thus the danger of the unwitting creation of the "I" as controller. "Although we do not meditate in our school," he says, "we do try to control our minds, not under special circumstances, but under all circumstances, and in each waking moment. ...When one meditates, one tries to control one's mind." Self-remembering does involve a certain focusing of the mind, but it is an open focusing, an alert stillness, an attention freed of fixation. One can speak of "control" but the pitfall is that one may also be postulating a controller-"I". Thus the identification with one's person is simply projected to a more subtle plane, that of the controller-"I." What Burton may have slipped into teaching is a form of mind-control such as is found in the 'teachings' of EST, Scientology, and Silva Mind Control.

With reference to the teaching, let three points be made. One, Gurdjieff gave his students a variety of meditative exercises. Two, not only is Burton's belief that meditation is a controlling of the mind so elementary as to be odd, it also demonstrates how little he understands the role of meditation in Work. Three, the notion that one can exercise control of the mind, as Burton says, "under all circumstances and in every waking moment" is an impossible ideal. Self-remembering requires energy of a very refined quality, and who can manufacture enough energy to remember themselves for sixteen consecutive minutes, let alone sixteen waking hours? Gurdjieff, himself, admitted that he couldn't do it. One must work for short times. As self-remembering becomes more organic, its duration and depth change, as to perceptions of time and space and the objects, gross and subtle, therein. Interestingly, Burton says nothing about a practitioner's realization that we do not remember ourselves but *we are remembered.* That is, there is no person to remember. It is grace, a gift. When one's attention is not subtle enough to see this, the work unavoidably is for the ego-I, the "spiritual doer."

Concerning being, Burton says, "The highest dimension of being occurs when one's self remembers to be." Again, which self? If he's referring to self-remembering initiated by the organism, this is only the second plateau of self-remembering, certainly not its highest level. Gurdjieff persistently spoke of our sleep, our mechanicalness, our lack of real being. Burton rarely mentions sleep or Gurdjieff's many negations of our ordinary beliefs about ourselves, such as our unquestioned possession of individuality, will, and the ability to do. Gurdjieff often made clear why this "negative" approach is necessary. It is not pleasant but it is fundamental to Fourth Way teaching. Burton presents instead a "feel good" approach which, interestingly, he buttresses by telling his students that he loves them. This is totally antithetical to Gurdjieff's teaching. And strangely, for all his proclamations of "love," Burton's prose gives the opposite impression. It is guarded, flat, and lacking not only in originality but in warmth and generosity.

So elementary is the overall discussion that questions begin to arise as to the actual quality and depth of Burton's experience. For example, anyone truly experienced in the practice of self-remembering knows it is a dynamic and fluid term which is world-specific; that is, the vibration of self-remembering in World 96 is not what it is in World 48, 24, or 12. One wishes Burton had made similar distinctions, as they would be supportive, at least in part, of his claim to have experienced what self-remembering means in "its highest form."

In the introduction to the book, a Burton student speaks of "verification," understanding, and "personal transmission." The juxtaposition of these ideas is worth a close look because the particular combination is one currently in vogue, often taken up and 'taught' by many who use it to justify their personal preferences and avoidances. The introduction proclaims that, "Because the Fourth Way is based on individual verification and understanding, as well as on personal transmission, each teacher reinterprets it anew. Robert Burton's teaching, while based on the knowledge transmitted by Gurdjieff and Ouspensky, has expanded to embrace...." This is actually an implicit admission that Burton has received no "personal transmission," but has only read books. (Many novice readers may miss this qualification.)

There is what is termed an "oral transmission" between teacher and student. Here the fundamental principle is "passed"—not in words but in silence. There is *no* interpretation *because it is wordless*. What *is*, and what is reflected, *is*. Interpretation occurs only when experience is reduced to thoughts. Re-interpretation occurs when the *form* of the original impulse of transmission has played itself out. Man number seven is the only one capable of giving a new form, a new face, to the teaching. Burton, in fact, claims to have the understanding of a man number seven. "You all do very well just to hear me. It is the discrepancy between a man number four and a man number seven, the discrepancy between your understanding and mine." That such a reinterpretation would be needed only a generation after Gurdjieff's death is dubious at best.

And even were it needful, the legitimacy of Burton's 'interpretation' is strongly suspect for two reasons. One, Burton never had a genuine Fourth Way teacher. And two, he has never submitted to the discipline and training of the Work. Burton finesses the question of legitimacy and lineage by positioning himself as a kind of Work-Gnostic who is in contact with a school on a 'higher plane' with astral teachers, and so, of course, he has had no need to study in a lesser, earthly school under a merely human teacher. Embarrassing questions involving core issues of esoteric transmission are thus deflected. Given the level of his recitations in *Self-Remembering,* and his lack of genuine connection with Gurdjieff's Fourth Way, one wonders whether Burton is actually teaching "Burton" under the guise of Gurdjieff.

The collecting of art plays a very large role in his 'reinterpretation.' Asked why he encourages art collecting, Burton explains that "Beauty produces its likeness in those who pursue it. This wonderful system stresses raising the level of impressions around one. Our school invests in art to strengthen the impressions octave." He also believes that "True art is founded upon transforming suffering, and a true artist is a world unto himself. Art is synonymous with one's self and there is no higher art form than one's own individual soul." This too is at odds with Gurdjieff who devotes a whole chapter in the *First Series* to art. Nowhere does he indicate that art "is founded upon transforming suffering" or that an artist is "a world unto himself." These are commonplace contemporary notions which stem from the post-Renaissance secularization of art and artists. Instead, Gurdjieff describes the deliberate, conscious process of creating objective art by the members of the club of the "Adherents of Legominism." Referring to the place of the arts in the life of the Fellowship of Friends, Burton says "It is interesting how we develop the habit of saturating ourselves with culture: the concert, this room, the music, the impressions, all these hydrogens are higher hydrogens. From this we try to create self-remembering."

Contrast this with Gurdjieff, who said, "Culture creates personality and is at the same time the product and the result of personality. We do not realize that the whole of our life, all we call civilization, all we call science, philosophy, art, and politics, is created by people's personality, that is, by what is 'not their own' in them." It should also be noted that work conditions at the Prieuré were intentionally made uncomfortable. The chateau was often not heated, and the meals, except for Saturday dinner, were meager. Compare this with Burton's penchant for lavish dinner parties, art collecting, opera-going, and the like.

BURTON'S BOOK POSITIONS HIM AS A CENTRAL FIGURE IN the spiritual world. Ingenuously, Gurdjieff ("A Greek-Armenian mystic and teacher of sacred dances") and Ouspensky are presented as equals, with Gurdjieff having cobbled together a teaching from various Eastern sources and taught it to Ouspensky. Gurdjieff, we are told, was master of the physical. Ouspensky, master of the intellectual. And now Burton is introduced as the master of the emotional.

Anyone familiar with what is known of the history of Gurdjieff's teaching will recognize the untruthfulness of this formulation. Gurdjieff brought an ancient teaching, complete and carefully reformulated for our time. Ouspensky, despite his assimilation of part of what Gurdjieff brought, and his recording that part as faithfully as he could, did not bring a teaching. Just as it can be seen that St. Paul, despite his illumination and labors, was not on a level with Jesus, so Ouspensky was not on the same level with Gurdjieff. Once this is recognized, the argument for Burton and his place alongside Gurdjieff and Ouspensky falls to pieces.

At times Burton departs so diametrically from Gurdjieff's teaching, that making any connection whatsoever is difficult. When asked, "Is our ability to self-remember controlled by the gods?" he replies, "Yes. One is paced through nine lifetimes, and each life is all that one can bear. Each person who enters the way will become immortal—that is why the way exists." Burton makes much of the gods. It would seem, given his many references, that his orientation is pagan. This would be in high contradistinction to Gurdjieff who never spoke about gods as such and had a high regard for Christianity (which he regarded as the purest of all teachings before it was corrupted). Burton goes on to prophesy, "Our school will produce seven conscious beings. Apollo [his school] will not reach its peak for centuries or millennia. Our school is one of the greatest schools in recorded history, and that is why suffering is so abundant." When his assertions are not vague, they usually are not verifiable. However, with apparent candor, Burton admits that "I still have considerable difficulty transforming negative emotions, primarily due to the violence of the suffering I must absorb to lift a school and humanity out of the chaos of impending hydrogen warfare." Only members of his school will survive the impending disasters of which he warns. (Recently, the hydrogen warfare prophecy has been replaced by earthquakes, certainly a more reasonable scenario given the many warnings by seismologists.)

Throughout, Burton's tone is an amalgam of the conventional seriousness of the plaster saint with the intellectual appreciator of art and nature who believes in his feelings. Perhaps he hasn't read what Gurdjieff says about feelings—*Faith of feeling is weakness...Love of feeling evokes its opposite... Hope of feeling is slavery.*

Though Burton is said to have suffered from obesity and addiction to Valium, he portrays himself as not having any serious struggles. Speaking of having "a little difficulty hearing the music tonight," he says, "A work 'I' advised me, 'You cannot speak if you cannot listen,' in a gentle, non-judgmental tone of voice. It was a third line of force for helping me to listen." Self-remembering begins with the shock of the realization that one has forgotten. Is "a little difficulty" a euphemism for forgetting himself? What was it that replaced listening? Contrast this with any of Gurdjieff's books, particularly the *Third Series*. In it, Gurdjieff reveals the depths of his despair at his failures to remember himself or convey his teaching, contemplates suicide, and realizes what he must sacrifice to remember himself and to have the energy to continue.

In a defining passage, Burton confesses, "During September 1967, I met Influence C through my first teacher. I have never been so impressed with anything else." Although Burton makes reference to his first "teacher," there's no need to mention the teacher's name since he was merely the instrument for contacting "Influence C." Burton makes much of his relationship with "Influence C," which he reifies into angels and gods with whom he is in direct contact. All of this he carries forward in a severely distorted form of Ouspensky's diagram of influences (which few people realize was invented by Ouspensky, not given by Gurdjieff who dismissed it without comment). Burton claims to speak to forty-four different angels, among them Jesus Christ and Benjamin Franklin. Now in his line of work one can understand talking to Jesus—but Ben Franklin? Odd, too, no mention of his channeling Gurdjieff or Ouspensky.

Burton, who allows himself to be deified by his students as "The Teacher," claims that two angels took him out of the body and enlightened him. In a 1981 interview, reporter Michael Taylor of the *San Francisco Chronicle* asked Burton if he thought he was Jesus Christ. Taylor said, "Burton stared for a long moment into the fire [in the fireplace] and then murmured: 'Thou sayest it.' The words, of course, are the reply of Jesus Christ to Pontius Pilate when asked if he was the king of the Jews. Taylor later asked Burton about Jim Jones and the suicides in Guyana. Replied Burton, "Mr. Jones was close to the gates of hell. We would hope we are close to the gates of heaven."

AS MENTIONED AT THE OUTSET, THE ONLY LIVING 'TEACHER' Burton has had, and this only for a short time, was Alex Horn. And Horn was a faux-Gurdjieffian. Burton, then, has made himself in his own image. Having a strong concentration and ego-will, Burton seems to have misrepresented and reduced the teaching to a Norman Vincent Peale mentalism by which all experience is interpreted through the medium of mind and imagination. By not working with and through the body, one intuits that Burton has unwittingly imprisoned himself within what he takes to be 'higher mind,' which is really the psyche, and so put himself at the mercy of its 'gods.' He puts a high emphasis on self-discipline and said, during the newspaper interview above, that he is proud of one incident in his life that illustrates the strength of his own self-discipline. "My mother was in a hospital and she was dying," Burton said. "They had to do open-heart surgery and I was in the fifteenth month of a sixteen month period of silence. I was denying myself speech. I saw her in the hospital and I did not speak. It was my aim not to speak."

The teaching is nothing to toy with. As represented by Ouspensky, it may seem simple enough but this is deceptive. Gurdjieff often warned that taking the teaching wrongly or only in part would make one "a candidate for the lunatic asylum." Having denied the body and controlled the mind, not surprisingly Burton's sexual center appears to be controlling him. From the Fellowship's very inception, Burton ruled that homosexuals were not allowed membership. Now a spate of lawsuits by former students for sexual exploitation have forced Burton to admit that he is homosexual. He is said to have seduced male students for many years by telling them he was an "an angel in a man's body."

BUT MORE SERIOUS AND SIGNIFICANT THAN ROBERT BURTON himself, his disguises, deceits, and level of understanding, is the question of whether or not his teaching is a reinterpretation or a distortion of Gurdjieff's Fourth Way, or worse, a deviation. In *The Reign of Quantity and The Signs of the Times*, the esotericist René Guénon maintains that the destruction of a teaching begins with its distortion, which prepares the way for a later deviation. The deviation, in turn, prepares for a "counter-initiation" whose effect, Guénon wrote, will be "the reign of what has been called 'inverted spirituality'...a parody of spirituality, imitating it so to speak in an inverse sense, so as to appear to be its opposite."

We do not presume to know who Burton is. Obviously, he must be an unusual and powerful personality with a special gift for promotion and organization. Whoever he is, a careful reading of his book and study of his life makes clear one thing: Burton is not—and never has been—in the Gurdjieff line. Thus, the 'reinterpretation' of the ancient teaching of the Fourth Way by Robert Earl Burton is, at the very least, a decided distortion.

Whatever happens to the Fellowship's founder, the professed "master of the emotional," whether he is retired, given a ceremonial post or canonized as a martyr, the day will come when the organization will have a new leader, no doubt squeaky-clean, who will command the "Ark of the Future." His will be a palatial and handsome headquarters full of valuable art objects, a budget in the millions, and a worldwide network of ardent tithing believers. The mistakes and errors pointed out here will be excised and the past reshaped. Thus a new generation of the idealistic and naive will have the challenge of discriminating between the esoteric and the pseudo-esoteric. But this is needful. The Fellowship of Friends has its place, its part to play, for as Gurdjieff said:

> The very idea of esotericism, the idea of initiation, reaches people in most cases through pseudo-esoteric systems and schools; and if there were not these pseudo-esoteric schools the vast majority of humanity would have no possibility whatever of hearing and learning of the existence of anything greater than life because the truth in its pure form would be inaccessible for them. Δ

Part III

The Mouravieff 'Phenomenon'

Though never taken seriously during his lifetime, and rarely mentioned in Gurdjieffian literature, the name Boris Mouravieff has in recent years threatened to become more than a footnote, thanks to a diligent campaign by his latter-day followers. A friend of Ouspensky's, Mouravieff first met Gurdjieff in 1920 in Constantinople and later moved to Paris. He never joined the Work, but was never quite able to get Gurdjieff and the teaching out of his system. He forever remained on its periphery, gleaning what information he could, always criticizing, casting doubt, standing between two stools. He kept up his friendship with Ouspensky and oversaw the editing and translation of In Search of the Miraculous. *After that, little more was heard from him. It was a surprise then in 1961, twelve years after Gurdjieff's death, that Mouravieff published a massive three-volume work,* Gnosis, *which claimed to be "the complete" exposi-*

tion of the exoteric, mesoteric, and esoteric tradition of Eastern Orthodoxy. Even more surprising was the fact that his book was a direct and unmitigated appropriation of the ideas of the Fourth Way as Gurdjieff had presented it during his Russian period (1912-1919), and which Ouspensky reported in Search. Essentially what Mouravieff did was to strip Gurdjieff's teaching of its mooring in sacred science and coat it with Eastern Orthodoxy, adding some peculiarities of his own making. There was, however, a glaring problem. The two teachings simply didn't fit together. Eastern Orthodox Christianity was mystical and monastic. The Fourth Way was scientific and rooted in ordinary life. Mouravieff surmounted this by inventing what he called "the Fifth Way"—a worldly celibacy of platonic courtly love between man and woman, "polar beings" whom he called "The Knight and the Lady of his Dreams." After Mouravieff's death in 1966 his book soon went out of print and the institute he founded in Switzerland, The Centre for Christian Esoteric Studies, came to nothing, closing its doors within two years.

What must be recognized is that Mouravieff, never having been a pupil of Gurdjieff's, bases his understanding of the teaching on that of Ouspensky—not Gurdjieff. And so, Mouravieff's understanding can only be intellectual and therefore partial. A refutation would be as unnecessary as it is tiresome were it not for a small band of Mouravieff's contemporary followers who, without providing any credible historical evidence, relying on hearsay and Mouravieff's personal conjecture and opinion as well as other biased sources, have mounted a campaign to: (1) discredit Gurdjieff, (2) deny the authenticity and origin of the teaching as Gurdjieff presented it, and (3) assimilate Mouravieff's "Christianized" Fourth Way into the Eastern Orthodox Church. Given this, it would be well to examine Mouravieff and the phenomenon he represents. We begin by exploring Mouravieff's relationship with Gurdjieff and then consider Mouravieff's teaching itself.

A RUSSIAN REFUGEE OF THE BOLSHEVIK REVOLUTION, BORIS PETROVITCH MOURAVIEFF WAS FIRST INTRODUCED to G. I. Gurdjieff in 1920 in Constantinople by P. D. Ouspensky. Mouravieff, two years younger than Ouspensky, was fascinated with the teaching, attended lectures and movements demonstrations, but formed a strong animus toward Gurdjieff. An aristocrat, intellectual and moralist, Mouravieff no doubt had trouble with Gurdjieff's unconventional behavior, his role-playing and trampling on people's corns, and of course his heavy Caucasian accent—an accent, Ouspensky said, putting it delicately, one associated with "anything apart from philosophical ideas." Should his behavior draw a reaction, Gurdjieff's way of teaching was to make the manifestation even worse, thus giving people the opportunity to observe their identification. Though Mouravieff was determined to stay "outside the zone of his [Gurdjieff's] personal influence," he had been "poisoned," as Gurdjieff would say, and could never entirely break away. For even after both men left Constantinople and located in Paris, Mouravieff continued to seek out Gurdjieff at the Café de la Paix and in Fontainebleau.

When Ouspensky broke with Gurdjieff in 1923 and asked Mouravieff to help with the translation and editing of his book, then titled *Fragments of an Unknown Teaching* (later retitled, *In Search of the Miraculous*), he gladly agreed. Thereafter, Ouspensky and Mouravieff exchanged many letters on the teaching and whenever Ouspensky visited Paris the two often had dinner together. These letters and meetings, Mouravieff said, "gave me the opportunity to discuss all the elements of the system with him." Thus, Mouravieff's understanding of the teaching could only have been founded on Ouspensky's understanding, not Gurdjieff's. To understand all of Mouravieff's subsequent thinking and actions, this point is crucial. Mouravieff apparently never saw it for he makes no defense of it. Or, perhaps, seeing that he could not defend against it, chose to avoid it.

The reason Ouspensky gave for his break with Gurdjieff was "to save" the teaching. Strangely, he was saving the teaching from the very man who embodied it. Given Mouravieff's judgment of Gurdjieff as "in the image of a fallen angel," he certainly supported, no doubt encouraged, Ouspensky's break. Though he had agreed to help Ouspensky with the book, obviously wishing to learn as much of the teaching as he could without coming under Gurdjieff's knuckle, Mouravieff strongly argued against *Fragments* being published. Of the last meeting he had with Ouspensky in 1937 Mouravieff wrote: "I was opposed to the publication. It seemed to me that esoteric doctrine, by its very nature, eludes an account described in detail by writing." Years later, with Gurdjieff and Ouspensky now safely dead, Mouravieff apparently had a radical change of mind. He came to believe that he had to 'save' the teaching from Ouspensky who had, of course, 'saved' it from Gurdjieff.

Mouravieff's first published attack on Ouspensky and Gurdjieff came in 1957 in a small magazine, *Edition Syntheses.* Biased and highly interpretative, it passed unnoticed. In 1961 he then began the publication of his 758-page, three-volume *Gnosis,* incredibly, all of its central ideas lifted directly from Ouspensky's book. First displacing the teaching by wrapping the Fourth Way in a heavy orthodox Christian coating, Mouravieff then distorted it by grafting on his own 'contribution.' This, a fanciful updating of medieval courtly love which he called the "Fifth Way."

Mouravieff's betrayal would certainly have stunned Ouspensky. Even more so, had he known how Mouravieff really saw him, since Ouspensky had considered him a close friend. For Mouravieff, Ouspensky was simply a likable person, talented as a writer but naïve, mystical and uneducated—someone very much his social and spiritual inferior. Mouravieff's 'Ouspensky' was, as he recounted, "charming—although subject to fits of passions—amiable, very skillful in dialectics, this was not a stalwart man. And then this was a self-taught person, he had not even finished his secondary schooling...."

An exiled aristocrat, Mouravieff had the typical sense of superiority over Russian emigrés he presumed were socially inferior, especially someone like Ouspensky, a high school dropout who "was not protected inwardly, by this precious armor which is *the scientific method*. Everything in him was wavering, therefore open to exterior influences." [Emphasis added.] Interestingly, this "unscientific" Ouspensky in his *New Model of the Universe*, cogently and critically discussed the views of Darwin and Einstein (both of which he rejected at a time when the world was completely entranced with these theories).

Ouspensky's was a rare nature, supremely rational, scientific, yet artistic, mystical. Formidable as his intellect was, he was open to feeling and intuition, and so could penetrate beyond what he called "the thin film of false reality" of ordinary life. Though certainly many levels above Ouspensky in terms of class and education, Mouravieff—as esotericist, thinker and writer—was simply not up to Ouspensky's level. Even a cursory examination of Mouravieff's writing shows it tends to verbiage and a lack of clarity and comprehension never found in Ouspensky's. One of Mouravieff's primary criticisms of Ouspensky is that his writing had "the character of reporting conceived in the style of the 20th century, that is to say with a strong personal nuance." This—the interweaving of the teaching with Ouspensky's own experiences—is exactly what has made Ouspensky's *Fragments* so compelling and given it such broad and lasting appeal.

Mouravieff went further, declaring: "On the whole, *Fragments of an Unknown Teaching* is nothing more than 'Gurdjieff as seen by Ouspensky.'" Exactly. Mouravieff unwittingly shows that his understanding of the teaching is predicated only on Ouspensky's. Also, to speak so condescendingly shows how little Mouravieff appreciated the brilliance, artistry, and intellectual integrity with which Ouspensky conveyed his experiences with Gurdjieff and his comprehension of the ideas.

Of this Ouspensky has said: "I have written down and described how we met the system and studied it. But I realized what a different impression it all produces on readers as compared to us who actually were there. A reader will never be able to find the right center of gravity....This is why there are no text books on the system. Things can be written only for those who have studied." It should be noted that Gurdjieff, aware of the difficulty in writing such a book, praised *Fragments* for its objective reporting of his presentation of the teaching prior to 1923. "Very exact is," Gurdjieff said. "Good memory. Truth, was so." And, "Before I hate Ouspensky, now I love him."

Mouravieff, always absolutely confident in his own interpretation, revealed a dimension of his relationship with Ouspensky he never suspected when he tells of the two dining with Baroness O. A. Rausch de Traubenberg, a friend who was helping to translate Ouspensky's book from Russian into English. The baroness' twelve-year-old son came to the table and asked that the two men write something in his album. Wrote Mouravieff: "Whatever happens in life, never lose sight of the fact that two times two make four." Wrote Ouspensky beneath Mouravieff's sentence: "Whatever happens in life, don't lose sight of the fact that two times two never make four." Ouspensky smiled, and gave Mouravieff a mischievous look.

The baroness, who knew both men well, shrugged her shoulders and looking from one to the other, said:

"Well!—in your maxims, I recognize you perfectly, you two."

Of this Mouravieff wrote: "Whim?—Certainly!—But from the point of view that interests us for the moment [Ouspensky's attitude toward life], Ouspensky was completely there." (Mouravieff was referring to here is what he saw as Ouspensky's chief feature—that he was too mystical and romantic, not scientific enough.)

Of course, Ouspensky, a real teacher in his own right, was not denying the rationality of two times two making four. Rather, he was completing Mouravieff's assertion. What he wrote took the absolutism of Mouravieff's statement (a feature of his) and reopened the statement for the baroness' son in the sense of raising questions about where and in what cases either of the statements is right or wrong, and further, in what instances they might both apply.

The understanding Ouspensky demonstrated in this episode was outside Mouravieff's categories of comprehension. Another feature of Mouravieff is that he appears to have always evaluated and interpreted from an ordinary scientific level within the context of very conventional notions of morality and good and evil. He no doubt had a strong intellectual center and he always wrote as 'one-who-knows.'

But what, in fact, did Mouravieff know?

Did he really know Gurdjieff? Know him well enough to judge him?

Did Mouravieff understand that Gurdjieff's mission was to establish the ancient teaching of the Fourth Way in the West and to do so as quickly as possible? That, according to Gurdjieff, unless a sufficient number of people awakened, the abnormality of the world, steeped as it was in self-love and vanity, would ultimately result in its self-destruction? That Gurdjieff's methods could sometimes be seen as harsh, even brutal, in their excising of false personality, but this was predicated by the exigency of the time and the hardness of its egotism? That, despite his knowledge and efforts, he could find no one willing to act as an instrument of the teaching, no one who could capably be "a helper-instructor"?

Mouravieff's negative judgment of Gurdjieff rests on four interpretations:

1. Gurdjieff's methods were "brutal"
2. Gurdjieff hypnotized his students
3. Gurdjieff's car crash proved he was not outside the Law of Accident
4. Gurdjieff stole the teaching.

The question of harshness or brutality has been partly answered. The heart of the matter is whether or not Gurdjieff was brutal in terms of essence and being, not just in his outward manifestation. Many of Gurdjieff's students have addressed this question, attesting to the rare quality of love that was his. One writes: "What I knew as a child, I am beginning to understand as an adult. Gurdjieff practiced love in a form that is unknown to almost everyone: without limits."

Did Gurdjieff hypnotize his students? Before coming to the West, he made his living as a professional hypnotist. He developed his knowledge and his *Hanbledzoin*, that substance upon which hypnotism depends to an extraordinary degree. Despite his oath not to use hypnotism—"I take an oath to remember never to make use of this inherency [telepathy and hypnotism] of mine...."—he found that "although I tried as much as possible...to keep under the control of my consciousness the undesirable manifestations of my nature, in spite of this, there gradually formed within me, proceeding far beyond the control of my active consciousness, certain automatic influences upon people around me during their waking as well as their hypnotic state. On account of this, there soon began to become really perceptible to my awaking consciousness various consequences, irreconcilable with my nature, of *this automatic influence over people*, which often evoked in me remorse of conscience...." [Emphasis added.]

What he is saying is that his presence was so great that, despite his keeping to his essence-oath, people still fell under this influence. We see the same effect with many, if not all, teachers of Gurdjieff's caliber. The projection onto the teacher, the unconscious miming of the teacher, the taking of his every manifestation as law, is simply a step on the path of the student which the teacher will break at the necessary moment. And Gurdjieff did. The nightmare train trip to Chicago with Fritz Peters, the bizarre pressures for money with Jean Toomer...these are simply two of the many instances that come to mind. One of Gurdjieff's intentions in the *Third Series* was to show himself to his students as a human being with human failings to keep them from idolizing him. How many teachers, one may ask, have had the courage and love to reveal themselves so unflatteringly? What we often see as Gurdjieff's weaknesses, and there were many as he forthrightly admitted, he painstakingly transformed into strengths by means of his uncompromising honesty about and struggle with himself.

Having placed and kept himself on the periphery, all of this was lost on Mouravieff. He wrote: "When a man from outside, like me, tried to raise a voice against the idolatry which ended with making of Gurdjieff a sort of Cagliostro or Rasputin, they looked at me with condescension, in fact with compassion."

Mouravieff made much of Gurdjieff's having said that when one enters onto the path, one frees oneself from the Law of Accident. He took Gurdjieff's car crash in 1924 and two subsequent crashes in later years as proof that Gurdjieff remained subject to this law. Mouravieff misinterpreted the crashes as instances of the Law of Accident to validate his view of Gurdjieff as having gone wrong.

The use of the word 'accident' as in 'car accident' does not necessarily mean the event was under the law of accident. For accidents, so called, occur under the law of fate as well. And Gurdjieff's 'accident' was a 'fated' occurrence. As Gurdjieff told Ouspensky, "Fate is better than accident only in the sense that it is possible to take it into account, it is possible to know it beforehand; it is possible to prepare for what is ahead. In regard to accident one can know nothing. But fate can be also unpleasant or difficult." Madame de Hartmann wrote of Gurdjieff's unusual precautions before the fateful drive: having the car thoroughly inspected and requiring her to travel back to the Prieuré separately. Clearly, Gurdjieff anticipated something interfering with his journey.

As mentioned previously, Mouravieff never understood Gurdjieff as having a mission, let alone the seriousness of that mission. For all his discussion of esotericism, Mouravieff never considered that Gurdjieff could be an avatar, a Messenger from Above, and that this, in itself, must evoke a corresponding denying force. Gurdjieff spoke of it as *Tzvarnoharno* and wrote that it "forms itself by a natural process in the communal life of people as an outcome of a conjunction of the evil actions of so-called 'common people' and leads to the destruction of both him that tries to achieve something for general human welfare and of all that he has already accomplished to this end."

A CENTRAL ISSUE IS MOURAVIEFF'S CONTENTION THAT Gurdjieff "stole" the teaching. Among his attempts to prove his case, Mouravieff wrote of an encounter with Gurdjieff that he believed was quite revealing, but, again, perhaps in a way he never supposed. One day seated with Gurdjieff at the Café de la Paix, Mouravieff asked him point blank:

"I find that the system is based upon Christian doctrine. What do you say to this subject?"

In French the sentence reads: *"Je trouve le systeme a la base de la doctrine Chrétien."*

There is an ambiguity in the way Mouravieff words his statement. It could be understood in two ways.

One, the system was at the base of Christian doctrine.

Two, the system was rooted in the Christian doctrine, the emphasis here being on "doctrine."

Why Mouravieff, who had been so careful in his phrasing elsewhere in his article, left this key phrase ambiguous remains a mystery. Perhaps he could not bring himself to misrepresent Gurdjieff so plainly?

Now to continue:

"It's the ABC," he [Gurdjieff] replied. "But they, they didn't understand at all."

The "they" referred to is presumably the Church fathers.

"Is the system yours?"

"No...."

"Where did you find it?—From where did you take it?"

"Perhaps I stole it...."

Given Mouravieff's negative judgment of Gurdjieff from their first meeting in Constantinople, it is inconceivable that Gurdjieff was unaware of Mouravieff's animus toward him. His answer, then, must be taken in the context of this knowledge. Mouravieff thought Gurdjieff stole the teaching, so Gurdjieff, of course, said that perhaps he did.

One can almost see Mouravieff smiling with knowing cynicism. And Gurdjieff, a master of the Way of Blame, intentionally drinking it in.

As for Gurdjieff agreeing with Mouravieff that the Fourth Way is based on Christianity—"It's the ABC," Gurdjieff said—Gurdjieff certainly never denied that elements of the Fourth Way could be found in the contemporary version of Christianity. He, in fact, says that "if only the teaching of the Divine Jesus Christ were carried out in *full conformity with its original* then the religion unprecedentedly wisely founded on it, would not only be the best of all existing religions, but even of all religions which may arise and exist in the future." [Emphasis added.]

For Gurdjieff—and this is an important point—the original Christianity which, as he said, the church fathers didn't understand at all, is *not the same* as contemporary

Christianity. This is because contemporary Christianity has been distorted and is, according to the *First Series*, in the last stages of the process of being destroyed. The original to which Gurdjieff refers has its origin in prehistoric Egypt. It is this original "Christianity" which is the ABC of *both* the Fourth Way and Christian doctrine.

So Mouravieff was asking and interpreting on one level and Gurdjieff replied from a much deeper level. Gurdjieff was certainly aware of this and fed Mouravieff's arrogance in thinking he could trap Gurdjieff, that he could see him, that he was on his level. As Gurdjieff once said, the "truth can only come to people in the form of a lie." Here, he told the truth, the deep truth, knowing full well that Mouravieff's interpretation of what he said would be only a half-truth.

Mouravieff, having read Ouspensky's book, was certainly aware that in Russia when Gurdjieff was asked about the relation of the Fourth Way to Christianity, he had answered: "*I do not know what you know about Christianity. It would be necessary to talk a great deal and to talk for a long time in order to make clear what you understand by this term.*" [Emphasis added.] But perhaps Mouravieff did not read closely enough. The use of the word "know" is meant in the sense of knowing as a component of being, the two together forming understanding.

Continued Gurdjieff: "But for the benefit of those who know already, I will say that, if you like, *this is esoteric Christianity.*" Because of the italicization of the words "esoteric Christianity" this is what draws the attention. But the operative, modifying words in Gurdjieff's answer are *know* and *if you like*. What Gurdjieff is saying is that—framing his answer in terms of the questioner's frame of reference, his level of understanding—the Fourth Way can be called "esoteric Christianity."

This, however, does not mean that the Fourth Way *is* esoteric Christianity. Nor does it mean that contemporary Christianity is the basis, the root, of the Fourth Way. The teaching is linked with Christianity, but in the sense that the teaching predated the origin of Christianity as we historically know it. "It will seem strange to many people," said Gurdjieff, "when I say that this prehistoric Egypt was Christian many thousands of years before the birth of Christ, that is to say, that its religion [the religion of prehistoric Egypt] was composed of the same principles and ideas that constitute true Christianity."

"The Christian church, the Christian form of worship," Gurdjieff declared, "was not invented by the fathers of the church. It was all taken in a ready-made form from Egypt, only not from the Egypt that we know but from one which we do not know. This Egypt was in the same place as the other but it existed much earlier."

These statements are as extraordinary and illuminating as they are radical. Perhaps they can be better understood if it is recognized that every real religion has two parts. "One part," Gurdjieff explained, "teaches what is to be done. This part becomes common knowledge and in the course of time is distorted and departs from the original. The other part teaches how to do what the first part teaches. This part is preserved in secret in special schools and with its help it is always possible to rectify what has been distorted in the first part or to restore what has been forgotten....This secret part exists in Christianity also as well as in other religions and it teaches how to carry out the precepts of Christ and what they really mean." The secret part, of course, to which Gurdjieff refers but does not directly name, is the Fourth Way.

What Gurdjieff said about the history of Christianity is equivalent to Copernicus saying that the sun and not the earth was the center of the solar system. Gurdjieff has said that people see the world "topsy-turvey," but the extent of the distortion is not often taken to be so radical. About the Fourth Way itself Gurdjieff also stated:

"Of the principal lines, more or less known, four can be named:

1) The Hebraic
2) The Egyptian
3) The Persian
4) The Hindu."

He then declared: "The teaching [Fourth Way] whose theory is here being set out is completely self-supporting and independent of other lines and it has been completely unknown up to the present time."

He said of theosophy and occultism that they can "give only negative results" because "they are a mixture of fundamental lines."

It follows then that the Fourth Way, elements of which are found in Christianity, as well as Sufism, the Kabbalah and so forth, *predates* these teachings. This cannot be stressed strongly enough. Exponents of each of these teachings have considered one or the other of them to be the origin of the Fourth Way, and propagandize to that effect.

To summarize: Mouravieff showed no understanding of Gurdjieff's approach. This he most clearly reveals in his shallow interpretation of Gurdjieff's *All and Everything, First Series*. In a word: he never got beyond boredom. He said he found the "reading of these pages without end...fatiguing." He did admit that the book had "perhaps some fifty interesting things," but, characteristically, they are not mentioned. For him the book was an "interplanetary narrative flood...a staggering heap with childish details." It recalled to him the novels of Madame Krzanowska, which were in vogue with Russian youth before the First World War. Even James Webb, Gurdjieff's first academic biographer, who for all his erudition and research never got to the heart of Gurdjieff or the teaching, nevertheless called Mouravieff's comparison "wrong" and "simplistic."

HAVING ADDRESSED MOURAVIEFF'S CRITICISMS OF GURDJIEFF, let us examine his criticisms of the Fourth Way. However, before beginning let us reiterate the all-important fact: *Boris Mouravieff was never in the Work.* Thus, his criticism and commentary, his understanding, can only be that of an outsider, one who is speculating intellectually, and based on his limited interaction with Ouspensky in his role in helping to translate and edit *Fragments.* What follows is a detailed dissection of the assertions of Mouravieff and his chief apologist Robin Amis. Untangling their web is difficult, requiring a careful reading, comparing what they say about their teaching with what Gurdjieff said and wrote, and verifying their statements by checking them against the sources they mention.

Essentially, Mouravieff makes three criticisms of the Fourth Way as presented by Gurdjieff:

1. Only fragments of the true teaching are given

2. There are important errors and deviations

3. These "errors and deviations of *Fragments of an Unknown Teaching* attest to the fact that the book was not written at the orders of, and under the control of, the Great esoteric Brotherhood [of Christianity]."

It will be shown, regarding the criticism of the teaching as fragmentary, that Gurdjieff's circumscribed presentation was intentional and an integral part of the teaching itself. As to its supposed errors and deviations, these are due to Mouravieff's misreading and misunderstanding. Lastly, there is the criticism that Ouspensky's book was not written at the behest of the Brotherhood. This will be taken up first.

The implication of Mouravieff's criticism of Ouspensky, though never explicitly stated, is that he himself writes under the direction and control of the Brotherhood. If so, why does he not say so directly? Would the claim subject him to too much scrutiny?

Since he says he is writing at the behest of the Brotherhood, then by that very "fact" we are to believe it must exist. How otherwise are we to know except by taking his word for it? The only support he gives for its existence is to quote an allusion of St. Paul's in his Epistle to the Romans, chapter 8, verses 28-30. The verses speak of a predestinate elect—those whom God has predestined "to be conformed to the image of his Son." Such predestination of certain individuals—certainly heretical in the view of the Orthodox Eastern Church—is one step of belief that Mouravieff asks us to take; that they meet and form a Christian brotherhood quite another. Of course it is possible, but possibility is no proof of actuality.

Robin Amis, editor of Mouravieff's writings and founder and director of an organization that promotes his thinking and publishes his books, has been under pressure to substantiate Mouravieff's claims. Struggling to do so, Amis writes that this Brotherhood's roots "lie in certain statements of St. Paul, *perhaps even Christ himself.*" [Emphasis added.] The words of St. Paul, of course, are open to many interpretations, but none clearly speak of a Brotherhood. If there is an esoteric Brotherhood one would think it must begin with Jesus Christ, so why the equivocal "perhaps even"?

Much of what Mouravieff is putting forth about an esoteric Brotherhood would be rejected by the Eastern Orthodox Church. Amis therefore is forced to mend fences. In a statement of negative intent, Amis tells us that Mouravieff's *Gnosis* because of "its specialist character...does not claim to be a work of Orthodox theology, nor to reinterpret Orthodox doctrine per se." Thus he signals that the ideas in the book do not threaten Orthodox doctrine and thus should cause no problem for the Church.

But why is this disclaimer necessary?

Of course, *Gnosis* is not "a work of Orthodox theology." What Amis cleverly denies, in fact, has never been claimed by Mouravieff. What Mouravieff *does* is make a positive statement of intent that his book is a "Study and commentaries on the *esoteric tradition* of Eastern Orthodoxy." [Emphasis added.]

To unravel this a critical distinction must be made— theology is one thing, the esoteric another.

Theology is the study of God and God's relation to the world. The esoteric is the operative, practical application of alchemical and spiritual principles which both the Latin and Eastern Churches have lost. (The medieval Cathars, later burned at the stake, spoke of this when they called their Catholic brethren "waterless canals.")

Both Churches would of course reject this. Faith, prayer and the keeping of the commandments they believe are sufficient. There is no need of the esoteric.

Another point: the terms "Eastern Orthodoxy" in Mouravieff's statement above means, of course, the Church. Mouravieff omits "Church" no doubt because his gloss on The Fourth Way and his representation of it in terms of esoteric Christianity would in no way be approved by the Church. In fact, if it gained acceptance, the Church would denounce it as heresy. So Amis' odd denial is an offering of appeasement, trying to forestall any undermining of Mouravieff's position.

Amis offers up another disclaimer when he further argues that Mouravieff is only expressing "ways of applying that [Orthodox] doctrine to *specific questions* of human spirituality." [Emphasis added.] By the word "specific," Amis suggests that the questions dealt with are not fundamental to spiritual transformation. Mouravieff's answers to these questions would, in fact, shake the Church doctrine to its very roots.

Mouravieff, himself, split no such theological hairs. For example, in his first volume he made the declaration that *Gnosis* gave the *"complete esoteric tradition* of Eastern Orthodoxy."* [Emphasis added.] The statement, out of keeping with the humility Mouravieff speaks about so admiringly, is so absolute in character (a feature of Mouravieff's previously noted) that Amis can do nothing but backtrack. He admits that Mouravieff's work "does not contain all the Christian esoteric teachings ever given." And in terms of Church doctrine, Amis also confesses that Mouravieff's version "does raise *sometimes challenging interpretations* of Theological doctrines." [Emphasis added.] As we have seen, Amis also has insisted that it is not an interpretation.

Does Mouravieff reinterpret Orthodox doctrine? Unquestionably. His reinterpretation of Orthodoxy is largely esoteric, taken as it is from Gurdjieff's teaching. What is based on his own views is often embarrassing. At the root of Amis' statements concerning Orthodoxy and Mouravieff is a cleverly contorted double-think that implodes on itself when logically unwound and scrutinized.

If Mouravieff's esoteric Brotherhood really does have its roots in St. Paul and perhaps even Christ, and if it can, as Amis contends, be "traced first through formative figures of the early churches" such as Clement and his student Origen, as well as to later saints like St. Basil, Gregory of Nyssa and Saint Simeon the New Theologian—what is the objection of the Orthodox Church? It would seem that the Church neither accepts nor condones Mouravieff's "Great esoteric Brotherhood." One must accept its existence, given the scant references, on the belief that Mouravieff himself has not become confused and is not acting from an animus of self-deception, anger, and ambition.

This question of the authenticity of Mouravieff's esoteric Brotherhood as "Tradition" has obviously given Amis a lot of trouble. In the second volume of *Gnosis*, Amis is forced to admit that Mouravieff is not speaking of "Tradition per se" (a distinction Mouravieff never made). Rather, Amis says it is "a particular Tradition handed down over centuries, in a *sometimes perhaps* broken line." [Emphasis added.] Amis buried the qualifying words "sometimes perhaps" in a footnote. Here he admits a significant fact: "There is evidence," he writes, "of this line's having been reconstructed or reconstituted several times in the past fifteen hundred years." In other words, Mouravieff's "Tradition per se," his "Great esoteric Brotherhood," died off and in being resuscitated was subject to many distortions. If it was ever connected with an esoteric school, which showed how to keep the precepts of Christ, that connection was lost. As Ouspensky once declared, "at a certain point religion may become cut off from schools. Particularly divisions of religion—first Christianity, second Christianity, third Christianity, tenth Christianity, and so on. Which has connection with school?"

Other than Gurdjieff, what are Mouravieff's sources? Before going into this, let us note that Amis finds it necessary to distinguish between Mouravieff's knowledge and his opinions "which, in obedience to his humanity, still do creep in here and there." Obedience to his humanity? Mouravieff makes much of the General Law of mechanicality from which one must escape. Passing off mere opinion as fact is indicative that one has not escaped but is rather still chained. Had Mouravieff been in the Work he would have been told he was engaged in formatory thinking, or worse, lying.

As to sources, the bibliography in volume two lists four pages of mostly Christian texts, two of the most important being the *Philokalia* and Clement's *Stromata*. Ouspensky, as every one familiar with him knows, was very much interested in the *Philokalia*. As he wrote in *The Psychology of Man's Possible Evolution*, "In early Christianity there was a collection of books of different authors under the general name of *Philokalia,* used in our time in the Eastern Church, especially for the instruction of monks." The *Philokalia's* decidedly monastic orientation puts much of what it says outside Gurdjieff's teaching, which is centered in a work in life, and the book contradicts Clement as well, who, according to Amis, is one of Mouravieff's "primary sources." Clement opposed a key feature of what we see later in Mouravieff's idea of the "Fifth Way"—*celibacy*.

Clement, speaking of celibacy for householders, "insisted it is better to marry and rise superior to the cares and temptations that beset married life than to be without the experiences that marriage brings." In the *Stromata* Clement is said to have attempted to unite Christianity, in which faith must come first, with Greek philosophy (though he was very much against the Stoic doctrine of divine immanence). Concerning Clement's *Stromata*, it is noteworthy that for Eastern Orthodoxy not Clement but his student Origen has been more influential. Said a commentator, "The history of Christian thought in the east from Origen's time on is largely the history of his ideas, that is, his ideas of God."

One can see the absolutist character of Mouravieff's thinking when comparing his views with Gurdjieff's. According to Gurdjieff, "Sexual abstinence is necessary for transmutation only in certain cases, that is, for certain types of people. For others it is not necessary at all. And with yet others it comes by itself when transmutation begins." And further: "If there is abstinence in one center and full liberty of imagination in the others, then there could be nothing worse. And still more, abstinence can be useful if a man knows what to do with the energy which he saves in this way. If he does not know what to do with it, nothing whatever can be gained by abstinence."

Celibacy, irrespective of the individual, is of course required at all the monasteries of Mount Athos. It is here that Mouravieff regards as being the center of the esoteric Tradition. He makes a great deal of this and yet sources are scanty. As Amis says, "Monks on Athos admit the existence of the 'Tradition' but say that it has never been fully spelled out in writing." Who these monks are and what they have told him of the esoteric Tradition, even if only in broad outlines, would be helpful.

In sum, a credible link between the Orthodox Church—be it on Mount Athos or wherever—and Mouravieff's "Tradition" appears dubious. Amis states that even Mouravieff admitted that the survival of this tradition "within the church is tenuous, that the doctrine does not appear to survive in full or has not been collected together in full." Another word for this is, of course, fragmentary. Ironically, Mouravieff scornfully accused Gurdjieff of presenting a teaching that was "fragmentary in character. In the esoteric realm, all fragmentary knowledge is a source of danger....Thus the incomplete is the source of all heresies." One could not more fully agree.

Let us now take a closer look at Mouravieff's criticism of the teaching as being fragmentary. Ouspensky's original title for his book, *Fragments of an Unknown Teaching*, is very likely at the source of Mouravieff's misunderstanding. A careful reading shows that the teaching Gurdjieff taught is anything but fragmentary, though, given Gurdjieff's method of teaching, it seemed so. Ouspensky understood this for he said, "In school one cannot begin with knowledge of all. So one begins with fragments. First one studies fragments relating to the psychological side, then fragments relating to man's place in the world, etc. After several fragments have been studied, one is told to try and connect them together. If one is successful, one will have the whole picture. And then one may be able to find the right place for each separate thing. There is no other way. One cannot learn the system from books." Ouspensky spoke of this in still another way: "In the beginning in Russia Mr. Gurdjieff always insisted that it was not a system; it was just fragments and one had to make a system out of them. And he insisted that it should be given in this way...it is taught in fragments each of which is on a different scale. You have to put them together and at the same time correct the scale. It is like several geographical maps, each on a different scale, cut into pieces. You have to see which piece fits which, where the scale is very different and where it is less different. This is the only way to study the system." It is clear from this that the word *fragments* had a very different meaning for Ouspensky than for Mouravieff. One was esoteric; the other ordinary. And from this confusion—aided and abetted by his animus toward Gurdjieff—what Mouravieff has wrought!

As great a book as is Ouspensky's, it is only a primer when compared with Gurdjieff's Legominism, *All and Everything (First, Second,* and *Third Series)*, which presents the complete teaching insofar as it can be given in words. Its unstated but unequivocal demand is that in reading the book the reader must first experience and absorb his fatigue, disillusionment, and whatever other psychological states may arise. To some extent, Mouravieff must have done this to be able to speak of the *First Series* as an "interplanetary narrative flood." But he never went further and so never penetrated to the deep esoteric teaching that lies within it. But how could he? He never surrendered to the demands of being a student of Gurdjieff's. In the Fourth Way, as Gurdjieff said, one initiates oneself, one puts all the fragments of the teaching together through the fire of one's observed and suffered experience, and so completes the teaching in oneself. Only a certain amount is given in this approach—it is up to the seeker to seek, question, verify, decrystallize and crystallize.

Now to turn to Mouravieff's criticism of errors and deviations. In terms of the errors in Ouspensky's *Search* (interestingly, Mouravieff never deals with *All and Every-thing*), the most fundamental seems to be Gurdjieff's statement (reported by Ouspensky) that man is said to be a machine, mechanical, and therefore only responsible for his actions when he begins to awaken. "The concept of the mechanical-man," says Mouravieff, "has as a consequence his irresponsibility. This is in direct contradiction to the doctrine of sin, repentance, and salvation which form the basis of the teaching of Christ."

For Gurdjieff, sin, repentance, and salvation are really experienced only by those who are on or are approaching the way of transmutation. That is, to sin one has to be in some sense awake, to know what he or she is choosing and not choosing. As for the concept of original sin, although Gurdjieff never speaks of it directly, it can be inferred that it is comprised of the egotistic consequences of the properties of the organ Kundabuffer which are passed by heredity from one generation to another. In sum, with regard to explaining sin, whereas Gurdjieff makes a distinction based on one's level of development, Mouravieff makes none. A careful examination of this difference gives a sense of a hierarchy of levels of understanding, from ignorant to esoteric.

Mouravieff also finds several of the diagrams in Ouspensky's *Search* "defective" while "others are missing." The comparison he makes is between the 1950 edition and the draft Ouspensky first gave him in the 1920s. Although Mouravieff made much of this, it is really a straw man. Does he actually believe that Gurdjieff—considering how deeply he buried the dog in *All and Everything*—would permit the publication of a book which let readers acquire all the ideas of the teaching without making any effort? That would be counter to a fundamental tenet of the Fourth Way—that the teaching is not given but attained. Once again, we see the workings of a mind which, despite its esoteric garb, is on many points decidedly literal.

Mouravieff gives two examples of defective diagrams. The first is the diagram of Influences and Magnetic Center (see *Search*, p. 204; *Gnosis*, Vol. 1, p. 51). Clearly, Mouravieff's diagram is more sophisticated. But he overlooks something. Ouspensky writes that at one of the meetings Gurdjieff "made me repeat what he had said about the way and about magnetic center." He then says, "I embodied his idea in the following diagram." To wit, the diagram does *not* represent Gurdjieff's understanding but Ouspensky's. Either at that time Gurdjieff did not give a full exposition, which certainly was in accord with the way he taught; or Ouspensky did not fully take in what Gurdjieff had said. If so, Gurdjieff would note this and create or take advantage of subsequent situations in which Ouspensky's error might be pointed out to him.

The second 'defective' diagram Mouravieff speaks of is the Diagram of Everything Living (*Search* p. 323; *Gnosis*, Vol. 2, p. 72). Here we know that Gurdjieff presented this diagram, for Ouspensky says, "G. drew a diagram in the form of a ladder with eleven squares." Of this diagram Mouravieff says: it "contains several errors. Most important is the place of man which in fact contradicts the theme of man's 'nullity'—it would have been better to say infinite smallness—that is expressed throughout that book, a theme which is fully in agreement with the Doctrine."

Gurdjieff says that man is part of organic life on earth, and of this organic life the evolving part is humanity. But within humanity only a part has the possibility to evolve. All men are necessarily machines. Simply by existing they mechanically fulfill a cosmic function of receiving and transmitting energies. Some have the possibility to evolve beyond this, that is, they may become conscious of their functioning and, in so making a conscious effort to remember and observe their functioning, may use a part of the energy and substance produced, the *Sacred Askokin*, for their own evolution, that is, to ultimately create a soul.

Ignorant of Being, all men are nullities, whatever their personal merits. It is only when men begin to awaken to Being that they step out of the dream of ephemeral egotism and begin to have true substance. The view that Gurdjieff brings is in conflict with the doctrine of contemporary Christianity which holds that all men have souls.

However, the point of the diagram is the transmutation of energies from low to high, high to low. In Gurdjieff's diagram we see three circles, each standing for a given 'hydrogen.' The lower circle shows that upon which a given class of creatures feeds. The hydrogen in the upper circle represents what class feeds on this class of creatures. The middle circle shows the average hydrogen which the given creatures represent. Thus man, hydrogen 24, feeds on invertebrates. And, in turn, is fed upon by archangels,

		GOD
		ARCHANGEL
SUPERMAN	SAINT	ANGEL
MAN		
MINERAL	PLANT	ANIMAL
METAL		
STONE		

Mouravieff's Version
of the
Diagram of Everything Living

hydrogen 6. There is a world of difference between mechanical and conscious eating, be it physical food, air, or impressions.

Mouravieff's diagram, by omitting the hydrogens, shows none of this. In his schema the hydrogens cannot be used because of his insertion of the Superman (a Nietzchean term hardly in accord with Eastern Orthodoxy) as a class of creatures and the elimination of the Eternal Un-changing, thus skewing the mathematical consistency of the diagram. It remains for the reader to ascertain which diagram is defective. Perhaps, here again, Mouravieff takes from Ouspensky who devoted a whole chapter to the concept in *New Model of the Universe,* and in turn took the idea from Nietzsche, whose viewpoint was anything but Christian.

Before leaving the subject of diagrams, it should be noted that Mouravieff says, "We all know the importance of diagrams in the Esoteric Tradition. They have been introduced to allow the transmission of this knowledge through the centuries in spite of the death of civilizations." If this is true of diagrams, why is it that when Mouravieff's sources are examined, such as the *Philokalia,* Clement's *Stromata,* and the writings of Gregory of Nyssa, St. Simeon the New Theologian, the Cappadocian Fathers, or more lately, St. Theophan the Recluse,

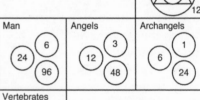

Gurdjieff's Version
of the
Diagram of Everything Living

we find no diagrams? Either there never were diagrams because these sources, as esteemed as they are, do not represent the Esoteric Tradition...or we are forced to take Mouravieff's word that they were passed orally. Because of the separation of time, whatever these early Christian sources said or did not say can only be Mouravieff's conjecture.

Lastly, let us examine Mouravieff's *Gnosis* itself. First, looking at Mouravieff's writing—even a cursory reading shows a level of consciousness well below Ouspensky's. That some would put Mouravieff on Ouspensky's level, much less Gurdjieff's, indicates the quality of understanding of those who do so. Moreover, so often in Mouravieff's use of Work ideas, words, and definitions, he takes from Ouspensky. For example, in speaking about buffers, he said they are, "like the buffers of railway carriages which soften shocks." Ouspensky defined buffers in this way: "We know what buffers on railway carriages are. They are contrivances which lessen the shock when carriages or trucks strike one another." It is a clear sign of immaturity, spiritual or otherwise, when one simply repeats the formulations of another without attribution.

In terms of content, within the first few pages of his first volume, Mouravieff writes about the doctrine of sin and the devil, gives the reader a breathing exercise, and, combining all this with Work ideas, then salts everything with biblical quotes. Later he will devote many pages to feminine beauty—he believes that what he calls "pre-adamic" women are more beautiful than the "adamic" and thus more tempting. He also devotes some thought to what might be called the esoteric fashion of the future.

What Mouravieff did, in essence, was take Ouspensky's version of the Fourth Way teaching, borrow most of its key principles and practices, Christianize them...and then, on this scaffold, erect at length what he calls "the Fifth Way"—a self-transformation through celibacy between "the Knight and the Lady of his Dreams." What Mouravieff offered is a Westernized form of unconsummated Rosicrucian-Tantric love between polar opposites, of the animus for the anima. Although linguistically antiquated, at least it *is* an esoteric idea. However, he could well have gotten it, as he got the teaching, from a book. Though there is no reason not to believe he practiced celibacy himself, there is no statement to that effect or any special clarity about his experiences of it in his writing. An intellectual, he wrote in terms of ideals and theories, not practicalities.

How far, indeed, Mouravieff went on his 'Fifth Way,' how much was speculation, how much experienced fact, cannot be ascertained. Gurdjieff also dealt with celibacy, or what he called "sexual abstinence." But he didn't make it the fulcrum of the Fourth Way. For certain types he said "a long and complete sexual abstinence is necessary for transmutation to begin." For other types he said "transmutation can begin in a normal sexual life." What Mouravieff has done then is to take one aspect and make it absolute. Furthermore, without long training or special conditions such as a monastery, for how many people can celibacy be a way of transmutation? And, when combined with the idea that the man, the Knight, must not only practice celibacy but also find a woman who is his polar opposite, the Lady of his Dreams, with whom to practice courtly love—when subjected to such critical examination—Mouravieff's way reveals itself for what it is: a romantic imagining that lacks a real basis in, and understanding of, human life.

What Mouravieff's *Gnosis* represents is not his understanding but his misunderstanding of Gurdjieff and the teaching. To take a fundamental example, Mouravieff took the Law of Seven as presented in *Search*, but he doesn't realize—though he claimed to have read the book—that Gurdjieff presented the materials for a much deeper understanding in the *First Series* in his discussions of this "fundamental cosmic sacred law" which he called *Heptaparaparshinokh*. (For those interested, see the fifth stopinder, the *Harnel-Aoot*.) That Mouravieff misses this outright is indicative of how much he missed and how his book is simply his personal elaboration of the Ouspenskian version of the teaching.

Besides the plagiarism and misunderstanding evident in *Gnosis*, there are also two curious omissions. Self-remembering and self-observation, the key practices of the Fourth Way, are never once mentioned. No doubt because the Orthodox Church, whose doctrine is based solely on remembrance of God, would find both terms noxious. For self-remembering, Mouravieff substituted a French word, rarely, if ever, used in English, *constantation*. This he defined as "to recognize the state of a thing or phenomenon, to establish a fact without applying any kind of personal judgment." Later, he expands the term's meaning by redefining a part of Gurdjieff's definition of self-remembering which has to do with the role of attention. Mouravieff said constantation "demands a *doubling* of attention; to the object, and to one's own self." [Emphasis added.]

However, Gurdjieff had defined self-remembering as a "divided attention," not a "doubled" attention. Mouravieff's mistaken reinterpretation is a serious distortion. For to *double* attention means to increase its force. This increase in force, in turn, requires a greater expenditure of energy which, unless there is a deep awareness, will certainly increase tension—organic, skeletal, and psychological. For all real work, a soft and relaxed body is necessary (otherwise the impressions hit like stones against a brick wall). Mouravieff's one-centered method, therefore, misses the mark.

To *divide* the attention, as Gurdjieff instructs, is *not* to increase its force but to work with the level of attention already present. One divides it between sensation of self and the perception of an object, exterior or interior. In so doing, what colors and personalizes impressions—imagination, identification, inner considering, and judgments—is observed. If one cannot absorb the shock of a given impression, there is immediate reaction followed by a train of secondary reactions. If the impression is registered and not reacted to—not fought, not expressed, not fed—then observation (what Mouravieff calls watchfulness) has duration and depth. The octave of impressions can proceed and its energy is further refined so as to be "food" for a higher body without which no true self-remembering (work with sensation and feeling) can begin to take place. In time a difference in quality is intuited between what is seen—the contents of one's awareness—and awareness itself. The ensuing friction created from the absorption of the energy of impressions and the denial of reaction produces an inner separation, an inner space.

Unlike Mouravieff, Amis does use the term self-remembering in his *A Different Christianity* in speaking of what he calls "the nonmonastic psychological method." He defines self-remembering à la Mouravieff as a "doubled attention." So even though Amis makes use of the term it is still defined incorrectly. It should be noted as well that time and again he mentions Mouravieff's unpublished writings to buttress some point. But since Mouravieff claimed that his *Gnosis* is "a complete exposition of the tradition," it is odd that Amis needs to resort to unpublished (and therefore not verifiable) writings. He also streamlines Mouravieff's definition of constantation by saying it is "perception without judgment."

Interestingly, in speaking of doubled attention neither Amis nor Mouravieff mention any equivalent to Gurdjieff's emphasis on (as reported in Ouspensky's *Search*) "the feeling of self," or the important role of sensation in self-remembering. The practice they propose is centered entirely in the intellectual center, not the body. The practice of constantation is particularly problematic for reasons which anyone who begins practicing self-remembering will observe: the mind is filled with judgments. Constantation, "perception without judgment," is a possibility only after one has learned to be *sincere* in the full meaning of this term.

After the inner taste of the distinction between impressions and reactions has evolved through long struggle with oneself, there appears an inner separation in which impressions, the reactions to impressions, and that which sees both is recognized. Emphasizing the seeing "eats" rather than "feeds" the reactions. One's seeing is thus direct, without the automatic filtering and coloring of judgments. Attention is free and clear, the mind still and supple. (One can see this state, for example, in the face and body of Michelangelo's statue of David.) But this state of vibration—let us for the while call it constantation—is not where one can begin. To believe one begins from this high state is simply to remain mired in the thought world where mental knowing substitutes for the ability to experience it.

Further, Mouravieff claimed that his psychological method is made up of three elements: prayer, doubled attention (a mental self-remembering), and constantation. Amis holds that the link—he believes there is a "missing link" between doubled attention and constantation—is prayer. This presupposes that one cannot come to constantation without prayer. This is not true. There is no need for prayer to still a mind that is already stilled through the division of attention, the creation of sensation and feeling and its discrimination, and ultimate resolution. How then can prayer be a "missing link"? Although prayer is not a link between the two, it certainly can help, especially when wordless, to deepen stillness while expanding the attention of mind beyond its self-imposed physical, emotional, and mental boundaries. (Let it be noted in passing that Gurdjieff's *First Series* contains many prayers and hymns.) But here we begin to entertain much deeper questions which move beyond the scope of the present discussion.

Why would Mouravieff not use the word *self-remembering*? Because to do so would—in the eyes of the Eastern Orthodox Church—totally invalidate his attempt at reconciling Fourth Way teaching with the doctrine in which there is only remembrance of God. The term is also dangerous in terms of doctrine because it may lead to the Self of Advaita Vedanta.

To examine Mouravieff's *Gnosis* in any greater depth would be beyond the scope of this inquiry, and indeed, to a greater degree, beyond the patience of the writer. A few last points, however, should be made.

At a recent conference, whose purported subject was Gurdjieff's *All and Everything*, Robin Amis was asked publicly to respond to Gurdjieff's statements about the origins of the Fourth Way, as cited previously. He declined to reply. Asked for evidence that the Fourth Way existed in Russian Orthodoxy and on Mount Athos, he spoke of Tolstoy and Dostoevski as being forerunners and held up an architectural drawing of a church on Mt. Athos which purportedly, by a stretch of imaginative interpretation, proved that the idea of the body having different centers, such as intellectual, emotional, and instinctive, was known. Hardly conclusive. He said that Gurdjieff on his death bed had instructed some of his pupils to go to Mount Athos. This, Amis claimed, was reported to him by two people who were present at the time. Who were these people? One was now dead, Amis said, and the other he could not name. Whether or not this statement is true, it is known that Gurdjieff directed some people to Mosul. Had there been a means of contacting prehistoric Egypt he undoubtedly would have directed people there. It is interesting, as well, that following Gurdjieff's death in 1949, his pupils visited Mount Athos. No contact was made with a tradition of esoteric Christianity. However, some thirty years later, Robin Amis claims to have made such a contact.

In conclusion, let it be said that Boris Petrovitch Mouravieff was a man of the past, a peculiar phenomena of his time.

There was no way, given his conditioning, that he could have ever recognized Gurdjieff, let alone judged him.

Gurdjieff came as a man of the future. He understood that, *historically,* as great as it once was, Christianity had played itself out. It was weighed down with the heaviness of time. While it might well have a resurgence it would be only temporary. To tie the teaching to its contemporary version would be to poison both.

How Mr. Gurdjieff "imported" the teaching, to use his word for it, and from where is not likely to ever be conclusively known.

What is important is the teaching itself. Δ

Epilogue

IF THE TRUTH BE TOLD, AND IT SHOULD, I DIDN'T LIKE WRITING THIS BOOK. I HAVE TRIED TO STICK TO THE facts and speak to the issues and not get involved in personalities. Yet what I have had to say is primarily negative. There is enough negation in the world. But taking with the left hand can go on only for so long before there is nothing left to take. At some point there must be an accounting; for to ignore, to be silent, is to affirm, albeit passively—not in one's own mind and heart but in that of others, those younger and more impressionable.

The time we live in is said by ancient texts to be the last of the four great cyclical ages. The Hindus called it the *Kali-yuga*, the ancient Greeks, the Iron Age. For both it is a time sick and confused with profane materialism. It was not always so. With the Golden Age, first of the cyclical ages, human life on earth was characterized by four essential qualities: *purity, austerity, charity* and *truth*. With every age, however, in the descending arc of time, one human quality after another was distorted then deviated...until it finally fell into its opposite. In the *Kali-yuga* only the last quality remains.

Whether or not the ancient texts could indeed be prophetic on so great a time scale, who can say? Yet certainly it can be seen that truth, however experienced, however conceived, undergoes relentless attack. Weakened and infected with pseudo-truth, so much of human life is materialized and personalized, marginalized, and manipulated—and all for what? In the name of what?

And as it is in the secular world, so too in the sacred. In particular, we see this leveling and devitalizing influence acting in the realm of the esoteric. Not only are inner teachings increasingly conceptualized and coated with personality, but there is little respect for the integrity of the teachings themselves, their approach, their language, and yes, their essence.

I remember a time years ago when several tribes of Australian aborigines on a worldwide tour came to Berkeley and performed their tribal songs and dances. I spoke to one of the aborigines afterward. Humanity shone in his eyes. He told me that once a year (I believe it was once) all the aboriginal tribes would gather and sing and dance. I asked if one tribe ever performed the songs and dances of another. "No," he said, bemused, as if the thought had never occurred to him, "our songs and dances are sacred. They have been given to us and are for us alone. Other tribes have their own and ours would do them no good."

That understanding we have largely lost. We take and use and combine and throw away and take again with rarely a thought as to what we are actually doing. Every part of the world, we think, is ours, all ours, and we can do with it what we like, especially if we can encapsulate it in words, ideas, systems. What is true of ordinary knowledge is especially true of the esoteric. The danger here is even more fundamental, for once the esoteric is mixed, its power personalized, what once gave freedom will then enslave.

Truth, sincerity with self, the last of the great human qualities under siege in our time, is what we must nurture and preserve in ourselves. We can only preserve that which we value. Preservation demands discrimination, an intuiting and distinguishing of the ascending from the descending, of what leads up and what down.

Years ago in New York I went into an old bookstore on Broadway, east of the Village, to buy Gurdjieff's *All and Everything*. I still remember the feeling of entering that bookstore, its silence and space, the shelves upon shelves of books stretching floor to ceiling, so high those at the top could only be reached by climbing a ladder. I remember my attention being drawn to a book by an author unknown to me. Instead of picking it up, as I normally would, I put the palm of my hand on the cover. My stomach felt queasy. For once I listened, and acted upon that listening, passing up the book and walking on, my eyes searching the shelves for the book for which my teacher had sent me. Δ

Selected Bibliography

Gurdjieff, G. I.

All and Everything
First Series: Beelzebub's Tales to His Grandson (Two Rivers Press, Aurora, Oregon, 1993)
Second Series: Meetings With Remarkable Men (E. P. Dutton and Co., New York, 1963)
Third Series: Life is real only then when "I am" (Triangle Editions Inc., New York, 1975)
Views from the Real World (E. P. Dutton and Co., New York, 1975)

Ouspensky, P. D.

In Search of the Miraculous (Harcourt Brace and Company, New York, 1949)
The Fourth Way (Vintage Books, New York, 1971)
A Further Record (Arkana, New York, 1986)
A Record of Meetings (Arkana, New York, 1992)

Pentland, John

Exchanges Within (Continuum, New York, 1997)

Nott, C. S.

Journey Through This World (Routledge Kegan & Paul, London, 1966)

Peters, Fritz

Gurdjieff Remembered (Samuel Weiser Inc., New York, 1971)

Collin, Rodney

The Theory of Celestial Influence (Arkana, New York, 1993)

Patterson, William Patrick

Struggle of the Magicians (Arete Communications, Fairfax, California, 1996)

Eating The "I" (Arete Communications, Fairfax, California, 1992)

Mouravieff, Boris

Gnosis (Praxis Institute Press, England, 1989)

Gurdjieff, Ouspensky and Fragments (Praxis Institute Press, Newbury, Massachusetts, 1996)

Amis, Robin

A Different Christianity (SUNY, Albany, New York, 1995)

A Search for Esoteric Christianity (Praxis, 1997)

Burton, Robert

Self-Remembering (Globe Press, New York, 1991)

Sherrard, Philip

The Greek East and the Latin West (Denise Harvey and Company, Greece, 1992).

Notes
&
References

Prologue

8   Unless the 'wisdom.' Fritz Peters, *Gurdjieff Remembered* (Samuel Weiser, New York, 1971) p. 122.

8   A day would come. Fritz Peters, *Boyhood with Gurdjieff* (E. P. Dutton, New York, 1964) p. 160.

12   Lord John Pentland. "The Teacher," as Robert Burton's students refer to him, is reported to have "commented that he [Lord Pentland] was a noble being, a mature man number four who was consistently trying to remember himself from the king of hearts, but a man in whom higher centers had not ignited." This comment shows the density of the commentator, for anyone who was open when meeting Lord Pentland could experience emanations of a rare quality. See Appendix I for a brief summary of the responsibility Lord Pentland was given by Gurdjieff. For how he worked with students, see my book *Eating The "I"*.

17   If a man merely 'thinks' of the Truth with his mind. Philip Sherrard, *The Greek East and the Latin West* (Denise Harvey and Company, Greece, 1992), p. 56.

18   Pseudo-esoteric schools. P. D. Ouspensky, *In Search of the Miraculous* (Harcourt, Brace & World 1949), pp. 313–14.

Part I: How the Enneagram Came to Market

All quotes of Helen Palmer from author's question and answer at Depot Bookstore, Mill Valley, California, 1988; "To Love and Work Better," *Moving Words* (February 1995); "Why the Enneagram, An Interview with Helen Palmer," *Gnosis* (Summer 1994); and "The Enneagram in Contention," *Gnosis* (Winter 1997).

All quotes of Claudio Naranjo from "A Report to the 'First Enneagram Conference' at Stanford University, 1994," *Enneagram Monthly* 2, no. 2 (February 1996); "The Distorted Enneagram," *Gnosis* (Fall 1996); and "The Enneagram in Contention," *Gnosis* (Winter 1997); also *Character and Neurosis* (Gateways, 1994).

All quotes of Oscar Ichazo from "I Am The Root of a New Tradition," *The Movement Newspaper* (May 1981); Michael J. Goldberg, "Enneagram Wars," *Los Angeles Weekly* (October 15, 1993); "Letter to the Transpersonal Community," *The Arican* (Summer 1992); "La Californie: Sectes bizarres, folies mystiques," *Le Figaro* (November 27, 1978). All reference to his early life is from "First Report on Arica Training in Chile" by John Lilly at Esalen (Big Sur Tapes, November 1970); John Lilly, *The Center of the Cyclone* (Julian Press, 1972); Francis Jeffrey and John Lilly, *John Lilly, so far...* (Jeremy P. Tarcher, Inc., 1990). See also "Report from Chile" by Claudio Naranjo at Esalen (Big Sur Tapes, May 1970); Charles Tart, *Transpersonal Psychologies* (Harper and Row, 1975).

All quotes of Kathleen Speeth from "Beyond the Enneagram," First International Enneagram Conference (Conference Recording Service, Berkeley, 1994).

"What Enneagram Tradition?" "Claudio Naranjo's living room," *Enneagram Educator* 5, no. 3 (Spring 1994).

21   Completely self-supporting. *Search*, p. 286.

21   The enneagram as a principal symbol of the Fourth Way. *Search*, p. 286. The closest representation extant to the symbol that Gurdjieff presented is to be found in Athanasius Kircher's (1601–80) *Arithmologia* published in Rome in 1665. Kircher, a Jesuit with a deep interest in Pythagoras and the Kabbalah, experimented with the effects of sound on matter and argued that the universe was based on sound as well as number and harmony. (See James Webb's *The Harmonious Circle* [G. P. Putnam's Son, New York, 1980], pp. 502–13.) Interestingly, Kircher was one of the first westerners who tried to decipher Egyptian hieroglyphs. Although he failed, he deduced, correctly, that the Coptic language was derived from the ancient Egyptian.

21   Universal hieroglyph. Ouspensky, *Search*, p. 294.

29   Seekers After Truth. "The Institute for the harmonious development of man by means of the system of Gurdjieff is, as it were, the continuation of the society known as the Seekers after Truth. This society was founded in 1895...." From the *Prospectus of the Institute for The Harmonious Development of Man of G. Gurdjieff*. Issued in October 1921.

30   Ichazo predicts a holocaust which will destroy the planet. In 1981 Ichazo was warning about climatic changes. "One of the worst dangers we are facing, is that the climate is going to change. The ionosphere has been hurt, and the danger is that climate

change not only threatens our outside being, but produces a change of all organic manifestation on our planet." Of course, at this time climatic changes were well known. In 1977 the *New York Times* said that the climate of the last forty years was abnormal in its normalcy and that the planet was entering a forty-year period where the climate would again become 'normal,' i.e., return to its chaotic conditions. As for change in organic manifestation, this was discussed by J. G. Bennett in his 1973 book, *Gurdjieff: Making a New World*.

30 Lilly uses LSD while at Arica. Early in his career, Lilly did some seminal work with dolphins, the results of which have been recorded in his three books on the subject. Possessed of a first-class scientific mind, Lilly's continual use of the drugs LSD and ketamine in order to transcend what he calls the "planetary trip," has led him to a series of strange prognostications and behaviors such as two extra-terrestrial powers, ECCO and SSI (good guys and bad guys), who fight for control of the earth. He once called the White House to warn of this and was briefly committed. He also believed that Eliot Richardson was controlled by the alien SSI. As Lilly admits, his emotional center is underdeveloped. He has difficulty relating to people and tends to mythologize women. Interestingly, ketamine, Lilly's drug of choice, is described as a "dissociative anesthetic," meaning that it allows one to separate from the feeling of pain, a process called analgesia. He is the scientist portrayed in the film *Altered States*. John Lilly, *John Lilly so far...* (Jeremy P. Tarcher, Inc., 1990), p. 175.

32 At the exoteric level. Ouspensky, *Search*, p. 311.

32 Gurdjieff movements stolen. Ichazo taught a type of Sufi dancing in Arica, according to Naranjo, that was somewhat similar to the Gurdjieff movements. Lately, what remains of Bhagwan Shree Rajneesh's, or Osho's, people teach a version of the movements. They say they learned them from the film *Meetings with Remarkable Men*. A large journal kept by Dushka, a student of Gurdjieff's, in which she copied the movements, was reportedly stolen from the archives of the Gurdjieff Foundation in New York.

37 Connecting chief feature with seven deadly sins. C. S. Nott, *Journey Through This World*, p. 87.

37 Astrological signs, compulsions, and typology. Fritz Peters, *Gurdjieff Remembered*, pp. 151–54.

40 Oral transmission. "Oral transmission, let us be clear, refers to personal, direct contact with a guide and community and to the entire set of conditions of living and human interaction established in the community." Jacob Needleman, *Consciousness and Tradition* (Crossroads, 1982), pp. 155–56.

41 There was no psychology then. Psychology, as Palmer understands it, is psychoanalysis, which is uniformly dismissed by all traditional teachings. For Gurdjieff it was a pseudo-teaching leading to a further deterioration of the contemporary psyche. Ouspensky saw in it "nothing of value." In its first stages, he wrote, it made "a series of very doubtful hypotheses and generalizations, [and] in the next stage it dogmatized them and in this way stopped any possibility of its own development." Its popularity "in certain literary and art circles and among certain classes of the public is explained by the justification and defense of homosexuality by psychoanalysis." See Ouspensky's *New Model of the*

Universe, pp. 271–72. Also see his *Psychology of Man's Possible Evolution*, First Lecture.

42 Ichazo's teaching filled with coined words. It is true that Gurdjieff used many exotic word formations himself, but this was only in the *First Series* of his *All and Everything*; one of its uses being to help train the attention. The terminology of the teaching is otherwise quite direct, such as identification, imagination, inner considering, inner separation and double crystallization.

42 Prehistoric Egypt was Christian. *Search*, pp. 302–03.

43 Nott writes about types. *Journey Through This World*, p. 87.

45 The cornerstone of the Fourth Way is objective reason, conscience and the unity of knowledge. *Search*, p. 278.

Part II: People of the Bookmark

All quotes of Robert Burton from Robert Burton, *Self Remembering* (Samuel Weiser, 1995); Michael Taylor, "A 'Holy' Teacher: Mystical Cult Prospers and Stirs Some Fears", *San Francisco Chronicle*, April 20, 1981. Jennifer Warren, "Trouble Taints a Cerebral Sanctuary," *Los Angeles Times*, November 11, 1996. Katherine Seligman, "Lawsuit Sheds Light on Yuba 'Church,'" *San Francisco Chronicle*, October 12, 1997.

47 The Fellowship of Friends. A number of former Burton students have started their own derivative organizations, such as the New American Wing, The Circle of Angels, and the London-based The Fourth Way™, whose founder employs Burton's bookmark merchandising, playing cards teaching and other devices. All offer a Burton-ized version of the Ouspensky version of Gurdjieff's Fourth Way teaching. Though like Burton's Fellowship,

each calls itself a Gurdjieff-Ouspensky teaching, in fact, only what is understood from Ouspensky's books is taught and Gurdjieff and his *All and Everything* is ignored. Nevertheless, all steadfastly claim to be authentic Fourth Way teachings.

48　**Tall, energetic, ambitious.** Lord Pentland made some pertinent remarks concerning this type of person in an interview he gave some nine months before he died. "Often the people who are best at organizing a community or school and who are best at making limitations (rules), the sensible ones," he observed, "are not those who are most serious in their inner search....Usually, the ones who are most sincere in their inner search are rather invisible to the public because they sometimes avoid positions of outer responsibility. They feel it will lead them into the marketplace." *Telos,* Vol. 2, Issue 4.

48　*A Canticle for Leibowitz.* Burton's idea of an ark which preserves the knowledge and culture of humanity during a dark age is taken from this book by Warren M. Miller, Jr., first printed in 1959. It is the science fiction story of the monks of the Order of St. Leibowitz the Engineer who, living in a monastery in the Utah desert, kept alive the ancient knowledge and so helped in humanity's rebirth from ashes after the Flame Deluge. The book's theme tapped into the prevailing psyche of the time—20 printings in 15 years—and Burton fulfilled readers' imaginations by promising to make the idea come true. Where once Burton spoke of the coming Armageddon presaged by a total world-wide collapse followed quickly by a nuclear holocaust, he now talks of a "catastrophic earthquake." This is a much safer 'prophecy' since seismologists have long predicted the coming of "the Big One."

48   17th century Chinese furniture. An ardent collector of museum-quality examples of craftsmanship and art for his Ark, Burton traveled the globe spending Fellowship moneys. A recent auction of Ming and Quin dynasty furniture at Christie's in New York City brought in $11.2 million, ten times pre-sale estimates. Burton is said to now be collecting 18th century French decorative arts. In the 1981 *Chronicle* interview Burton was asked about why he collected art. "'Beauty produces its likeness in those who pursue it,' Burton says. The idea behind how he inculcates this beauty in what he calls 'my students...my children' is that one's level of consciousness can be raised through an appreciation of beauty and materialism, 'the finer things of life.'"

49   Rodney Collin. Burton, who found Gurdjieff's esoteric writings too obtuse, focused instead on the books of Ouspensky and Rodney Collin. He took Collin's theory of human body types, given in *The Theory of Celestial Influence,* and elaborated upon it.

49   Alexander Francis Horn. Not much is known about Horn, but, according to the *San Francisco Chronicle*, his dinner-theater 'Fourth Way school' operation, known as the Theatre of All Possibilities (the name taken from the Herman Hesse novel, *Steppenwolf),* had an income of $40,000 per month or some $500,000 a year. Of this, $20,000 was from student dues and $20,000 from the sale of theater tickets. Students, required to sell tickets to the weekly productions, were harangued and physically beaten if ticket quotas were not met. At Horn's instigation, all-night drinking marathons culminating in fist fights were common occurrences, all in the name of the teaching. Punishment, in many forms, was a feature of Horn's teaching. A local drama critic

wrote, after sitting through three hours and leaving at the end of Act II of Horn's three-act play, *The Fantastic Arising of Padraic Clancy Muldoon*—"In more than ten years of reporting on the local theater scene, I remember no more punishing experience." Burton had long before been dismissed from the group, but this gives a portrait of Horn's psychology and his approach.

49 The student has to find the teaching. "And first of all, it [the teaching] has to be found. This is the first test." *Search*, p. 46.

50 Self and awake. When later in Burton's book a student asks, "Do the higher emotional and higher intellectual centers constitute the self?" Burton replies, "Yes." But Gurdjieff and Ouspensky rarely refer to the self. *The Guide and Index to the First Series* (The Society for Traditional Studies, Toronto, 1971) gives one listing of the word "self," unhyphenated. The word appears only three times in *Search*. Almost always the word is the first part of a compound such as "self-remembering," "self-observation," "self-will," or "self-love." The word is used to refer generally to the whole of a person, whatever their level of understanding, and not just the two higher centers. In Advaita, the Vedantic teaching of India, the word is capitalized as in "Self" and is taken in its absolute sense.

50 Highest form. As long as something remains within a form, even at its highest, most subtle expression, it remains within the world of form. But true experiencing begins with the formless. Otherwise, no matter how subtle, the experiencing remains in the subject-object world of dualism of form, there being the subtle perception of object, say of blankness, and that which perceives the perception of such, the sub-

ject. Pure perception is perception without a subject, without a knower. The question emerges then: how can there be perception without a perceiver? How can it be known that an object is perceived without a subject to perceive it? This question presupposes that consciousness is within the subject and not the subject within consciousness. The "I" appears within consciousness. Consciousness does not appear within the "I," it only seems that way because of the unconscious identification with the "I," the knower of the moment. Those who are strongly identified with the mental insist on knowing. Whatever the experience, they unconsciously insist on retaining the knower, and so forever stay within the confines of the known, of duality.

51   The work must begin from personality. *Search*, p. 248. See also p. 163, and the discussion of chief feature.

53   An impossible ideal. G. I. Gurdjieff, *Third Series, Life is real only then when "I am"*, p. 19.

54   Man Number Seven. According to Gurdjieff's Fourth Way teaching, the evolution of man is divided into seven steps. Man number one is predominately ruled by the body; two, by the emotions; and three by the intellect. All are "asleep" to themselves. This is the level of mechanical humanity. Only man number four is beginning to wake up to himself and beginning to balance his body, emotions and intellect. Man number five is a man who has reached unity which has crystallized. Man number six is very close to man number seven but differs only in that some of his properties have not as yet become permanent. Man number seven "means a man who has reached the full development possible to man and who possesses everything a man can possess, that is, will, consciousness,

permanent and unchangeable I, individuality, immortality...." *Search*, pp. 71–74.

54 'Personal' transmission. Burton's use of the word "personal" is another indication he hasn't had a teacher. What is transmitted is experienced as impersonal.

55 Dubious interpretation. For example, Burton has invented a deck of cards as a metaphor to represent centers and parts of centers by which he "reinterprets" Gurdjieff's teaching. It boils down to a shorthand labeling formula, which, like other work-derived personality or body typologies, lends itself well to "solidification" and abusive usage by individuals obsessed with power and control. Gurdjieff, although he wrote and spoke of types in many different contexts, refrained from codifying them in a system which could be exploited indiscriminately by people at lower levels of being. The only exception to this rule was his toasts to the "Idiots." But by enshrining the types as "idiots," he made sure the typology wouldn't be abused—referring to someone else as an idiot puts them on guard and makes it difficult to convince them of one's noble motives.

55 Burton never had a genuine Fourth Way teacher. Burton's *only* teacher was Alex Horn who was never in the Gurdjieff Work. A martial arts expert and actor-director with a dramatic flair, Horn learned of the Fourth Way teaching through his second wife who spent a number of months in J. G. Bennett's International Academy of Continuous Education at Sherbourne, England. For information on Alex Horn see "Theater Group: Cult or Stage?" by Jack Brooks, *San Francisco Progress*, December 22, 1978. Horn is criticized for financially exploiting his students and subjecting them to psychological abuse, even beatings.

See also "Real-Life Drama in S. F. Theater Group," by Michael Taylor and Bernard Weiner, *San Francisco Chronicle*, December 23, 1978. The story focuses on allegations of "beatings, child neglect and a student fee structure that yielded huge revenues."

55 Burton is actually teaching "Burton." According to former students, little mention is made of Gurdjieff. Ouspensky and Nicoll are emphasized because their level of development and logical discourse make little esoteric demand on the reader. One former student said that Burton had her read the *First Series* so she could provide him with glosses.

56 Adherents of Legominism. G. I. Gurdjieff, *First Series*, pp. 449–523

56 The whole of life created by personality. *Search*, p. 162.

57 What Gurdjieff says about feelings. *First Series*, p. 361.

58 Ouspensky's diagram of influences. *Search*, p. 204.

59 Burton and his mother. A reader replied to Burton's story about not speaking to his mother on her death bed, saying: "I have worked with a number of people who have had direct contact as pupils with Ouspensky and—more importantly—with Gurdjieff himself. To respond to the incident of silence with his [Burton's] dying mother, my understanding is to be internally free of our negatives, fears, and considerations. To be able to respond to the needs of the moment and to give up his own in face of something more important takes real strength—not the misdirected effort which he claims to represent as the teaching. I must state these people are not followers of Gurdjieff or Ouspensky, but of Burton, and that speaks for itself."— Marilyn Wurtzburg, Berkeley, California. *San Francisco Chronicle*, October 12, 1981.

59   Taking the teaching wrongly or only in part. We see this with the so-called enneagram movement of Helen Palmer who believes the "oral tradition" of the enneagram was passed on to her by Claudio Naranjo, who Oscar Ichazo exiled for grandiosity. Using the enneagram as a personality tool is akin to taking confession from Catholicism and thinking you have something. Though the enneagram first appeared in the West through Gurdjieff, his role has been diminished and both Ichazo and Naranjo are now held, according to their clique, to be the "fathers of the personality enneagram." Former Gurdjieffian Kathy Speeth, who left her teacher Lord Pentland for the arms of Naranjo in the 1970s, now disowns the enneagram movement she helped to create, as does Naranjo. But with scores of books and newsletters and the 1994 First International Enneagram Conference at Stanford having drawn 1,400 people, the popularization and debasement of the esoteric symbol continues unabated. However, there may be a flagging of interest, as the Second Conference held August, 1997 at the University of Maryland drew only 500 people.

59   Consequence of reducing and misrepresenting the teaching. "But in consequence of the wrong work of centers it often happens that the sex center unites with the negative part of the emotional center or with the negative part of the instinctive center. And then, stimulation of a certain kind of the sex center, or even any stimulation at all of the sex center, calls forth unpleasant feelings and unpleasant sensations. People who experience unpleasant feelings and sensations which have been evoked in them through ideas and imagination connected with sex are inclined to regard them as a great virtue or as

something original; in actual fact it is simply disease." *Search*, p. 258.

60   Plagued with a series of lawsuits by former students.
Besides the financial exploitation of members, Burton has been accused of seducing male followers,
single and married, as well as young boys. He does
so under the guise of being an angel—"I promise
you I am an angel in a man's body"—declaring that
he represents Influence C. (This is a very refined
vibration whose origin is esoteric and has many
manifestations. Any identification or imagination
in regard to such an influence immediately distorts
and aborts its elaboration.). A former secretary and
chauffeur of Burton's who once was in charge of
one of the Fellowship's centers said, "The Fellowship is a dictatorship, a predatory dictatorship. I
should know. I was a leader." Though married, he
succumbed to Burton's sexual advances. "He said I
had to be close to him," said the former student of
eighteen years, "that I had to submit my will to my
teacher. I just remember walking around in a daze,
smiling and feeling like I wasn't alive anymore. I
was in a state of shock, like a robot." A spokes-
woman for the Fellowship accused the former secre-
tary-chauffeur of mounting a "vendetta" against the
Fellowship and suggested he take responsibility for
his actions and "get on with his life." Another student who joined the Fellowship when seventeen
years old said that same year Burton invited him to a
"teaching dinner," plied him with alcohol and assur-
ing him he was really an angel seduced the young
man into a sexual relationship which continued spo-
radically for the next eight years. [See Seligman,
"Lawsuit Sheds Light..." *San Francisco Chronicle*,
October 12, 1997] Continuing lawsuits by former
students have forced Burton to admit his homosexu-

ality. Ironically, from the beginning he denied homosexuals membership in his organization.

60   Destruction of a teaching begins with distortion of it.
René Guénon, *The Reign of Quantity and The Signs of
the Times* (Penguin Books, 1972), p. 321.

Part III: The Mouravieff 'Phenomenon'

All quotes of Boris Mouravieff, unless otherwise indi-
cated, derive from the article by Boris Mouravieff, "Ouspensky, Gurdjieff and Fragments of an Unknown
Teaching," *Editions Syntheses*, 1957. It has since been published as *Gurdjieff, Ouspensky, and Fragments of a Forgotten
Teaching* (Praxis, 1997). Also from his book *Gnosis*, Vol. 1,
2, and 3 (Praxis Press, Newbury, Massachusetts 1989).

64   Knight and Lady of His Dreams. It is wondered
whether Mouravieff's esoteric knowledge really
lies with the Rosicrucians and Freemasonry, both of
which were very strong among the aristocracy of
pre-Bolshevik Russia. In Maria Carlson's essay
"Fashionable Occultism: Spiritualism, Theosophy,
Freemasonry and Hermeticism in Fin-de-Siècle
Russia" in the book *The Occult in Russian and Soviet
Culture* (Cornell University Press, 1997), she writes:
"Masonry freely adopts elements from a variety of
religious systems and creates a diverse system of
rituals. It emphasizes the concept of a mystic
'Quest' and uses terminology of knighthood as a
central metaphor for its strong initiatory features,
which are constellated in a central pageant of figu-
rative Death, Resurrection, and Rebirth and
expressed through a complex system of arcane
symbols." And in a footnote continues: "The
images of knighthood, quest, beautiful lady, etc., so
prevalent in Russian Symbolism [a movement of

poetry, prose and arts derived from the French Symbolists such Rimbaud, Baudelaire, Verlaine, Huysmans] derive from many sources: revived literary and artistic interest in the medieval period, interest in the Arthurian legend, renewed interest in courtoisie, the mystic operas of Richard Wagner. But another, completely overlooked source of such imagery was speculative Freemasonry, which claims a chivalric origin; perhaps even more relevant is the symbolism of its Rosicrucian variant, or emblematic Freemasonry."

65   Mouravieff first introduced to Gurdjieff in 1920. That Ouspensky had known Mouravieff before Constantinople is unclear. Two years younger than Ouspensky, Mouravieff was born in Kronstadt, the naval base at St. Petersburg, and was raised and educated in St. Petersburg. Given his interest in esoteric subjects, he might have met Ouspensky at the Theosophical Society, or possibly Mouravieff attended one of Ouspensky's public lectures at the Duma. What seems more certain is that they did not meet at bohemian clubs like The Stray Dog that Ouspensky frequented, for Mouravieff's father was Graf Piotr Petrovitch Mouravieff, admiral of the Russian fleet and vice minister of the Russian navy in the last imperial government before Tsar Nicholas II's abdication. Mouravieff himself was Prime Minister Kerensky's principal private secretary during Kerensky's service as the second prime minister of the new Russian Republic. Previously, he had been an officer in the Russian navy.

66   Mouravieff strongly argued that Fragments not be published. Had Ouspensky published the book, it seems clear from Gurdjieff's later praise of it that it could have created the bridge with which the two

men might have reconciled, either then or when Ouspensky returned to England from America in January 1947. Its publication would also have provided the teaching with a much needed impetus. So Mouravieff supplied a negative critical influence that had deep repercussions.

67 This was not a stalwart man. It is interesting to note Mouravieff's sentence construction and usage of "this was not a stalwart man" in which he uses the impersonal "this was" to raise himself above and distance himself from his subject.

68 Written for those who have studied. P. D. Ouspensky, *A Record of Meetings*, pp. 118–19.

70 Gurdjieff practiced love. *Gurdjieff Remembered*, p. 160.

70 Did Gurdjieff hypnotize his students? *Third Series*, p. 25.

70 Certain automatic influences upon people. G. I. Gurdjieff, *The Herald of Coming Good* (Sure Fire Press, 1988), p. 64.

71 Proof that Gurdjieff remained subject to this law. He ascribed this to Gurdjieff's mocking of God, but there is absolutely no evidence of this. Even a casual reading of *All and Everything* will show Gurdjieff's deep reverence for God. What he did mock was the institutionalization and polluting of Christianity.

71 Fate is better than accident. *Search*, p. 164.

72 *Tzvarnoharno*. G. I. Gurdjieff, *Herald*, p. 12.

72 Seated with Gurdjieff. His language "seated with" shows both his distance from and the equality he believes he has with Gurdjieff.

72 I find that the system. In the Praxis edition the translation is: "I find the system is basic Christian Doctrine. What have you got to say about that subject?"

73 The best of all existing religions. *First Series*—the original edition, p. 1009.

73   Mouravieff's animus. Gurdjieff was under no obliga-
tion to say what he really meant for a number of
reasons. Though declining to be a student of
Gurdjieff's and having an animus toward him,
Mouravieff thought he still had the privilege of
asking questions. He assumed an understanding
and level of being equal to that of Gurdjieff, i.e.,
Mouravieff could see who he was and judge him.
He is "poisoned" in the worldly way and Gurdjieff
simply pours him a full glass of truth which no
doubt was later a great help in bringing Mouravieff's *Gnosis* into the world so that later discriminating generations could see, if they wished, the
sources of Mouravieff's confusion.

74   "Christianity" has its origin in prehistoric Egypt. In
time Mouravieff perhaps came to realize what
Gurdjieff was telling him, but, of course, in terms of
his own coloring. Well-versed in the teaching as
presented during Gurdjieff's Russian period (1912–
1919), thanks to editing Ouspensky's book, it is no
surprise that he, too, dated the teaching, or "the
message," back to ancient Egypt "and from there to
time immemorial." His intention was to root its
modern manifestation in what he called "oriental
Orthodoxy," and in the esoteric teachings of the
antique world following a path through primitive
Christianity "up to and including the Slavs and the
Scythians and Byzantine-Russian Orthodoxy." As
he gave no evidence to substantiate these claims,
one is left at sea. But given his bias, that of rooting
the Fourth Way in Russian and Eastern Orthodoxy,
there can be no ready acceptance of his lineage.

74   Esoteric Christianity. *Search*, p. 102.

75   True Christianity, *Search*., p. 302.

75   Not from the Egypt that we know. *Search*, p. 286.

75 The secret part is the Fourth Way. *Search*, p. 304. In the early days of Gurdjieff's Institute for the Harmonious Development of Man at the Prieuré, Gurdjieff said: "The program of the Institute, the power of the Institute, the aim of the Institute, the possibilities of the Institute can be expressed in few words: *the Institute can help one to be able to be a Christian.* [Emphasis added.] He then continued, "There were Christians long before the advent of Christianity" and explained that "A Christian is a man who is able to fulfill the Commandments." See G. I. Gurdjieff, *Views from the Real World*, pp. 152–54.

76 Completely unknown up to the present time. *Search*, p. 286. Hence, those who try to combine Fourth Way practices and ideas with Theosophy dilute and distort the ancient teaching Gurdjieff brought and give life to a 'teaching' that can only lead people to "negative results." Gurdjieff's position on Theosophy and occultism is unequivocal. "...there are many things worse than 'black magic.' Such are the various 'occult' and theosophical societies and groups. Not only have their teachers never been at a school but they have never even met anyone who has been near a school. Their work simply consists in aping. But imitation work of this kind gives a great deal of self-satisfaction. One man feels himself to be a 'teacher,' others feel that they are 'pupils,' everyone is satisfied. No realization of one's nothingness can be got here and if people affirm that they have it, it is all illusion and self-deception, if not plain deceit. On the contrary, instead of realizing their own nothingness the members of such circles acquire a realization of their own importance and a growth of false personality." *Search*, p. 227.

76   Completely self-supporting and independent. *Search*, p. 286.

76   About *All and Everything* being an initiatory text. The noted esotericist and egyptologist R. A. Schwaller de Lubicz, spoke of the Pyramid Texts in a way that could be ascribed to Gurdjieff's lego-minism. "The purpose of initiatory texts is far less a logical one than it is to provoke shocks, emotional reactions, or to grate against the cerebral need for sequential logic. Paradox, improbable images, the juxtaposition of unconnected phrases are freely employed. The texts appeal to sensation, to a feeling of emotive sensitivity." R. A. Schwaller de Lubicz, *Esotericism and Symbol* (Inner Traditions, Rochester, Vermont, 1985), p. 58.

76   Mouravieff's comparison "wrong" and "simplistic." After publication of his book *The Harmonious Circle*, Webb became seriously morose and ended his life by shooting himself in the head.

78   Conformed to the image of his Son. *Romans 8:28–30.* "And we know that all things work together for good to them that love God, to them who are called according to his purpose. For whom he did fore-know, he also did predestinate to be conformed to the image of his Son, that he might be the first born among many brethren. Moreover, whom he did predestinate, them he also called: and whom he called, them he also justified: and whom he justi-fied, them he also glorified."

78   A Christian brotherhood. It is of course true that in the *Second Series, Meetings with Remarkable Men,* Gurdjieff speaks of brotherhoods such as the Ess-enes, the 'World Brotherhood' and the Sarmoung Brotherhood which he says "according to tradition, was founded in Babylon as far back as 2500 B. C."

And in the *First Series* he speaks of brotherhoods such as the Heechtvori and Brotherhood-Olbogmek.

78   The editor of Mouravieff's writings and founder of an organization. Robin Amis' Praxis Institute puts out a correspondence course on esoteric Christianity, including monographs and other materials in support of its assumptions. The publisher was greatly influenced by Jacob Needleman's nonfiction work *Lost Christianity* (Doubleday & Co., New York, 1980) which he mentions in his introduction to *Gnosis*, Vol. 3. He never seems to have realized the identity of Father Sylvan, the book's central figure.

78   Perhaps even. Boris Mouravieff, *Gnosis*, Vol. 2, Robin Amis' Introduction, pp. xiii–xiv.

78   The words of St. Paul. Interestingly, Ouspensky said, "I don't think he was a school man." *A Record of Meetings*, p. 135.

79   Specific questions of human spirituality. *Gnosis*, Vol. 3, Robin Amis' Introduction, p. xv.

77   Mouravieff's "Great esoteric Brotherhood." Which is not to say that there may not be one. The question is whether, in fact, Mouravieff made contact with it.

81   Religion may become cut off from schools. *A Record of Meetings*, p. 519.

82   Origen's ideas of God. Arthur Cushman McGiffert. *A History of Christian Thought* (Scribner's, 1932), p. 230.

82   It is better to marry. *A History of Christian Thought*, p. 188.

82   Clement is one of Mouravieff's primary sources. For the Catholic Church Clement's orthodoxy is questionable. Thus his name was omitted from the martyrology of Pope Clement VIII and later confirmed by Pope Boniface XIV. Pantaenus, Clement's teacher, is thought to be trained in Stoic philosophy

and Clement himself had a great fondness for Greek philosophy. He believed that Greek philosophy, though pagan, "provides for the soul the preliminary cleansing training required for the reception of faith, on which foundation the truth builds up the edifice of knowledge." (See Clement's *Stromata*, Book VII, p.33.) He held that the devil is endowed with free will and that the goodness of God is voluntary, it being a matter of will and not of nature. Also, not only did he oppose celibacy but the doctrine of original sin is thought to have played no part in his thinking. The Eastern Orthodox Church also finds Clement's views a bit disconcerting and clearly favors those of Clement's pupil Origen. Thus, Mouravieff's choice of Clement as a primary source for his thinking would seem to put him at variance with both churches.

82   Sexual Abstinence. See *Search,* pp. 256–57.

83   The incomplete is the source of all heresies. Clement, *Stromata* Vol. 1, p. xviii–xix, (Garland Publishing, New York, 1987).

83   One cannot learn the system from books. *A Record of Meetings*, p. 118. From a meeting December 7, 1936.

84   The system and fragments. An important distinction indicative of levels of understanding. Ouspensky and Mouravieff refer to the system, whereas Gurdjieff speaks of the teaching, as in "The teaching whose theory is here being sent forth...." *Search*, p. 286. In P. D. Ouspensky's *The Fourth Way,* p. 400–01, he reported: "In the beginning in Russia Mr. Gurdjieff always insisted that it [the teaching] was not a system...it is taught in fragments..."

82   Mount Athos. A rugged tongue of rock and land jutting into the sea in northern Greece, Mount Athos is regarded as the holy mountain of Eastern Ortho-

dox Christianity. For the past millennium, the whole peninsula has been a site for monastic settlements involving sprawling compounds, hundreds of smaller houses and hermits' hideaways. There are twenty monasteries on Mount Athos which have kept alive a tradition of study and liturgy. At its apogee, Mount Athos had some 40,000 monks. That number today has dwindled to 2,000. Mouravieff's connection to Mount Athos is through a relative, Andre Mouravieff, who, as a member of the Holy Synod (the ruling body of the Russian Orthodox Church) and a chamberlain at the imperial court, founded the monastery of Saint Andrew there in the 1800s. It has been deserted since 1926 because of a plague.

84   Ouspensky's book is only a primer. As Sri Anirvan pointed out, Ouspensky's book only spoke of the first two stages of the Work. "He remained silent about the last two because he had left Gurdjieff....The writings of Gurdjieff, on the other hand, open for us the frontiers of the two last stages. These are cleverly hidden in mythical narrations." Lizelle Reymond, *To Live Within*, (Doubleday & Co., 1971) p. 194.

85   Man is said to be a machine. *Search*, p. 19–20. Ouspensky asks Gurdjieff if a man is responsible for his actions and Gurdjieff answers, "A man is responsible. A machine is not responsible." Later, p. 357, he makes a further distinction. "Sins are what keep a man on one spot if he has decided to move and if he is able to move. Sins exist only for people who are on the way or approaching the way....Sin is what puts a man asleep when he has already decided to awaken."

85   Properties of the organ Kundabuffer. The organ Kundabuffer, the origin of egotism, was implanted

in man by a commission of Sacred Individuals who reasoned that man would cause much trouble if he came to prematurely know his true situation. It was later removed but the consequences of the properties persist. Original sin in man came from without. Man bears no intrinsic blame.

85 A straw man. Madame Ouspensky sent Gurdjieff a few chapters of the book in 1948 and, given their quality, he authorized publication. He did know that Ouspensky was writing a book, as Ouspensky had asked for permission to do so in Constantinople.

86 Embodied his idea in the following diagram. William Patrick Patterson, *Struggle of the Magicians*, (Arete Communications, 2d ed. 1997) p. 27. Ouspensky says: "Our ordinary European logical method of thinking makes us inclined to accept everything literally...Eastern thought, however, often uses methods of exposition totally different from ours. Eastern authors often do not define their subject as a whole. They are apt to give only one instance of the possible meaning of the given subject or phenomena without saying that it is merely an instance so that readers are left to understand their words as they like or as they can. Gurdjieff very often did the same thing."

86 Evolving part of humanity. *Search*, p. 306.

88 The importance of diagrams in the Esoteric Tradition. *Gnosis*, Vol. 1, p. xviii.

89 Buffers on railway carriages. *Search*, p.154.

92 The feeling of self. *Search*, pp. 118–19.

93 Gurdjieff and Prayer. See *Gurdjieff Prayer Book* (Arete Communications, Fairfax, California, 1997)

95 Christianity had played itself out. As one of many current examples, see "Rock (Music) of Ages: Monterey crowd testament to growth of Christian

sound," *San Francisco Chronicle*, August 2, 1997. As Plato said in *The Republic*, "Any musical innovation is full of danger to the whole State...when modes of music change the fundamental laws of the State always change with them." Consider this in terms of the music of the last fifty years or so: from Frank Sinatra to Elvis Presly, Col. Parker's "white niggra," to Heavy Metal to Rap to the Christian sound. [We take the Beatles, Dylan and the early Moody Blues, etc., to be lawful but short-lived correctives—this manifestation was too high to sustain because it was based not on hard practical work on oneself but on a tab of acid. The "highs" were artificial, created what Gurdjieff would call "imagination in higher emotional center" and subject to psychic pollution. In connection with what is likely to come, see D. H. Lawrence, *Apocalypse* (Penguin, 1976) and René Guénon's *The Reign of Quantity and The Signs of The Times*, from chapter 24 on.

Appendix I

131   I came to nothing. *Telos*, Vol. 2, Issue 3.

Appendix IV

145   Comments on St. Theophan's translation of *Unseen Warfare*. See St. Theophan's *The Heart of Salvation*, p. 77 (Praxis Institute Press, Newbury, MA, n.d.) edited with commentary by Robin Amis. *The Heart of Salvation* is based on extracts from *Raising Them Right* (Conciliar Press, Ben Lomand, CA). It was originally titled *The Way of Salvation*. A second book is *The Path to Salvation: A Manual of Spiritual Transformation* (St. Herman of Alaska Brotherhood, Platina, California, 1996)

Appendix V

148 Schools of a religious nature. *Search*, p. 5.

148 Is not my way. *Search*, p. 375.

149 New Testament in German. *Maurice Nicoll: A Portrait* by Beryl Pogson (Globe Press, New York, 1987) p. 95.

149 You must go. *Struggle of the Magicians*, 2 ed., p. 209.

Appendix I

John Pentland

In a beautiful riverside cemetery in Valhalla, New York, on a hillside by a tall spreading tree stands an unusual gravestone of granite. Carved into the rose-tinted stone is a design, medieval in style, of two entwined dragons' bodies, one with a lamb's head, the other a wolf's. Between the two heads is a fish looking as though it had just escaped from water. The heads and fish forming a triad, the whole symbol in granite is enclosed by a Celtic interlacing of lines. The inscription reads:

Lord John Pentland 1907-1984

And below this the admonition:

Commit thy work to God.

This is the last earthly statement, so fitting, of the man G. I. Gurdjieff chose to lead the work of the Fourth Way in America. Shortly before he died Gurdjieff told the then forty-two-year-old Lord Pentland, "You are like Paul, you must spread my ideas." And that he faithfully did. President of the Gurdjieff Foundation in New York from its inception in 1953, he was also the founder of the Gurdjieff Foundation of California. He was instrumental in the creation and development of study groups in various cities and during his lifetime personally acted as a teacher to hundreds of students seeking to genuinely awaken from the automatism of ordinary life.

Not only did he help to spread the teaching, Lord Pentland forever strove to preserve it in its original form so that its real value and power as a sacred way could be passed on to later generations. As Gurdjieff taught, in time all is deflected from its original course if not adequately resisted, and in Lord Pentland's day—as ours—the predominant deflections took the form of syncretism, eclecticism and other isms. These he stood resolutely against and for that was cast by some as being too doctrinaire. But he was a warrior in the best sense of the term, and personal considerations, such as the dislike or disagreement of others, never dissuaded him from the task he had been given.

To understand the task's significance it is important to recognize what the Fourth Way was for Gurdjieff. The teaching, he held, actually *predates* the four principal ways: Hebraic, Egyptian, Persian and Hindu. It is "completely self-supporting and independent of other lines," he declared, "and it has been *completely unknown up to the present time.*" [Emphasis added.] Certainly elements of the teaching are found in other ways but this is the result of deflections, not the opposite. The teaching has also been linked to esoteric Christianity for when asked about the teaching's relationship "to Christianity as we know it," Gurdjieff answered, "if you like, *this is esoteric Christianity.* But he is not referring *only* to contemporary

Christianity. For later he makes the astonishing statement: "The Christian church, the Christian form of worship, was not invented by the fathers of the church. It was all taken in a ready-made form from Egypt, only not from the Egypt that we know but from one which we do not know...*prehistoric Egypt was Christian many thousands of years before the birth of Christ.*" [Emphasis added.]

Gurdjieff had fulfilled his mission of bringing the teaching to the West—unless the wisdom of the East and the energy of the West could be harnessed and used harmoniously, he had warned, the world would be destroyed. Now the aim was to spread the teaching, a task for which Lord Pentland was uniquely prepared. Born Henry John Sinclair near London in 1907, he lived from the ages of five to twelve in India where his father served as Governor General of Madras. At eighteen he inherited the title of Lord Pentland and studied engineering at Trinity College, Cambridge. He traveled widely and had entered the worlds of politics and business when in 1937 he first heard P. D. Ouspensky's lectures on Gurdjieff's teachings. He studied with Ouspensky and his wife Madame Ouspensky at Lyne Place outside London and later, when the Ouspenskys moved to America, at their estate at Mendham, New Jersey, undergoing twelve years of arduous preparation on both the theoretical and practical sides of the teachings by two of its prime expositors. After Ouspensky's death, he said, "it became clear to me that even after all those years with Ouspensky I hadn't arrived at anything: I came to nothing." This recognition of one's nothingness—"The recognition," as he says, "that almost everything that has been normally regarded as hope is misunderstanding"—is in fact the necessary precondition for the real ignition of being and is, contrary to its appearance, the essential fulfillment of the aim of sincere work on oneself. So presenting himself to Gurdjieff, he received the direct transmission of the teaching, and was charged with his life's task.

As Gurdjieff was for Lord Pentland, Lord Pentland was for his many students—the primary spiritual influence in their life. Now, with the publication of *Exchanges Within* (Continuum, New York, 1997) containing selections from meetings he led in California, 1955-1984, a new generation of seekers may be introduced to an inspiring level of self-sincerity and keenness of observation. Of course, what no printed word can convey is the extraordinary penetration of the man's consciousness, his being. As with all great teachers, there was a potency in these meetings that radiated throughout. An unprepared reader, one whose attention still tends to be totally identified and who is not therefore receptive to more subtle levels of vibration, approaches this material, as it were, "dry"—having no inner support other than his own interested attention. His task—keeping his attention on what he is reading—is made no easier in that, while the material has been selected and arranged to achieve a certain purpose, it has only been lightly edited. Little to no translation has been made in reducing the living experience of the spoken word to the printed word. The resulting demand may so erode one's ordinary interest that one is stripped to the bedrock of their "raw attention." This, in itself, if recognized, is an experience of great value. As Lord Pentland responds to a questioner, "You see you are unable to bring all of your attention onto what you're reading. Can you follow that or not? You see that while you are reading you're thinking about something else." So just in the sense that Gurdjieff's Legominism *All and Everything* creates conditions in which to experience the material, the reader must first experience himself, the same is true of *Exchanges Within*. The "meat" of the Work is here. As Henry Leroy Finch, former professor of philosophy at Sarah Lawrence College and CCNY states in his foreword, this volume takes its place alongside those of Thomas Merton, Simone

Weil, Martin Buber, Frithjof Schuon and D. T. Suzuki as one of the "genuinely valuable modern works of spiritual direction and guidance."

Faced with a book of this quality there may be an impulse for the reader to "force-read" the book, in the grip of the usual mechanical idea, as Lord Pentland says, that "'I' must do it." This will lead to no new point of view. Rather, he advises that, if possible, readers come to a sensation of themselves: "You have to be in some way related to this presence in yourself and also related to what you are doing." In having this wish, one may eventually come "to a particular quiet, a kind of quiet that we receive rather than create or make." Of course, as this approach to reading is *not* automatic but intentional—it cannot be maintained for long. To a questioner, Lord Pentland suggests making such an effort for ten minutes. For a reader not practiced in working with attention it will be notably shorter—but of real value—for as Gurdjieff said, "No effort is wasted."

Everything, as Gurdjieff has also said, has two ends. Referring to this *quiet that we receive,* Lord Pentland points out that we must also learn to create this quiet for ourselves, for "If you haven't learned enough about it to create it for yourself, you will grasp at it in whatever framework it arises. If it's an object, or person or a book—not understanding how this quiet arises, you will want to possess the book or the person or the object." The profundity of such a perception, so simple on its surface, can only come from a deep and sustained work of attention that has moved so far beyond the ordinary idea of temptation as to give a small reflection of the true meaning of the term *esoteric.* For the careful reader *Exchanges Within* abounds with such insights.

Questioner: Will I ever be able to learn this? [Speaking about the teaching as it is presented in Ouspensky's *In Search of the Miraculous.*]

Lord Pentland: You have to repeat. Through repeated readings of *In Search of the Miraculous,* you have to be able to listen to the places where one idea is related to the next one in that book. The whole point is in the relationship, where he's [the author] speaking about one idea and then he goes on to the next. It's the juxtaposition of those two ideas which is the central point. And that includes all the tables. And of course it's the same thing, only more so, much more so, in *All and Everything,* But in that sense, these books are themselves teachers. Until you can understand the sequence, the relationship between one idea and the next one, you haven't got very far."

Exchanges Within is just such a teacher, a work of attention, for those who would be taught a very ancient way of awakening while remaining in—and creatively transforming—our experience of ourselves and everyday life. Δ

—William Patrick Patterson

Reprinted *Telos* Journal, Vol. 3, Issue 2
& *Gnosis* Magazine, Fall, 1997

Appendix II

Letter From a Former 'Bookmark' Student

The letter which follows arrived from Dublin, Ireland shortly before this book went to the printer. It is published with the permission of the sender, who wishes to remain anonymous.

Dear Telos,

I read the review of Richard Burton's book [in *Telos*] and thought it was quite accurate, After reading it and Patterson's books I had to acknowledge a decision that I was coming to in spite of myself, namely to leave the FOF [Fellowship of Friends] and seek something else.

One point of disagreement: The review points to a lifestyle of opera and lavish dinners for FOF members and contrasts this (unfairly I think) with the harsh conditions that existed at the Prieuré. In reality many FOF members in "Apollo" lead quite a frugal existence, working long hours, and if they do attend a fancy dinner they will more than likely have spent many hours helping and serving at many other such dinners. Also, staging an opera is by and large an opportunity for members to work together and maybe learn something.

Having said this, Burton's emphasis on art appreciation and absorbing "refined impressions" from it has never made much sense to me. Nowhere, in any of Gurdjieff's or Ouspensky's books is this mentioned. Peculiarly, this same notion of "refined impressions" attracts many to the FOF and makes them feel quite comfortable there. Some imagine themselves as aristocrats of a sort.

I don't know if you are familiar with Burton's use of cards. The King of Hearts represents the intellectual part of the feeling center and according to Burton is the gateway to higher emotional center. He says exposing oneself to art, music etc. develops this part of oneself and so aids evolution. You'd be amazed at the number of members who consider their "center of gravity" to be the King of Hearts. The notion of developing the King of Hearts through art and "refining one's alchemy" is one of the cornerstones of Burton's teaching.

In contrast to this is the King of Clubs, who represents the intellectual part of the instinctive center. This is the least popular "card" in the FOF and is often used synonymously with "false personality." Thus the instinctive center and false personality tend to be viewed together.

One result of this is that Gurdjieff's (who is perceived as being "instinctively centered") writings are rarely if ever mentioned, especially by Burton. This contrasts with Ouspensky, who is often quoted. As such, many members of the FOF, although drawn initially by Gurdjieff's ideas, become uncomfortable with Gurdjieff.

The most striking idea for me in Patterson's books is that Gurdjieff was a "messenger from above" as Beelzebub says. I never thought of Gurdjieff as an "avatar" and the idea had lodged in me that his teaching was incomplete and a composite he put together himself. This arose from reading various books by people involved with Ouspensky and Gurdjieff. For instance Nott paints a gloomy picture of Ouspensky, and Bennett explored many other teachings after the death of Gurdjieff.

I hadn't considered that Gurdjieff left behind a living teaching. I read a book a few years ago by David Kherdian and he presented the Gurdjieff Foundation in a poor light. Also writers like Colin Wilson and Robert DeRopp give the impression that while Gurdjieff was unique, his followers remained much as they were and the teaching wasn't effective for them. A book by Raphael Lefort (Idries Shah) gives the notion that Gurdjieff cobbled together his ideas from Sufi sources and that people doing Gurdjieff's exercises and movements were wasting their time, the "time and place" now requiring something different. And of course in the FOF, Burton maintains that Gurdjieff's teaching died with him and that this was symbolized by the light going out at Gurdjieff's funeral. After a time, these attitudes affect one's outlook whether you're aware of it or not.

Then along came *Eating The "I."* It brought to the surface many misgivings and questions I had about the FOF. The review of Burton's book only further confirmed and gave expression to my questions.

So I have decided to leave the FOF in the new year. One of the hard parts about leaving is losing contact with people one has gotten to know over the years. Former members are anathematized in the FOF, so current members are reluctant to keep in contact. This is one reason why many fear leaving, especially if they have put "all their eggs in one basket", the other being a Burton instilled fear of losing "C influence." Δ

Appendix III

Amis' Search

Apparently Robin Amis' talk on Gurdjieff at the Bognor Regis conference did not succeed in his own mind, for almost immediately thereafter he published a monograph, *A Search for Esoteric Christianity*, in which he states that "I had insufficient time to gather enough data, and even less time to present it. The presentation I made at the conference was therefore seriously incomplete."

The excuse of "insufficient time" is at variance with the facts as Amis himself presents them. He claims to have made contact with an elder of the esoteric tradition on Mount Athos (who has since died) as early as 1983. After which he edited and began to publish in 1989 Mouravieff's three-volume *Gnosis*. By 1995 he had written his own 388-page book on the subject, *A Different*

Christianity. Thus, the data, what there was of it, was already available. This is confirmed in that his monograph mentioned above reports nothing of importance which he had not previously published.

Amis' primary mistake is, like Mouravieff's, to not look deeply enough into Gurdjieff's remark when he says in a reply to a question about the relation of the Fourth Way to Christianity that "...if you like, *this is esoteric Christianity.* (See the Prologue for a discussion.) Amis, like Mouravieff, so wants something to be true that he makes it true for himself and then goes about trying to convince others.

He does his best to try to show that Christianity and the Fourth Way are one and the same. While there are some similarities, of course, they are quite different. He finds, for example, that "esoteric Christianity taught a form of self-remembering—which it called *nepsis*: sometimes translated watchfulness." But just as the bare attention practice of Buddhism is not self-remembering neither is watchfulness. Had Amis used the term self-observation rather than self-remembering he would have been closer to the mark, but even this word has its own special meaning. (See Jean Vaysse's *Toward Awakening*, Far West Undertakings, 1978.) While one is first asked to practice a simple form of self-observation, it is later shown that only by adding the practice of self-remembering can one really begin to observe oneself. Amis perhaps might argue that he said that esoteric Christianity "taught *a form* of self-remembering," but this is merely linguistic parrying. [Emphasis added.] It is interesting, as well as indicative, that he speaks of Gurdjieff and Ouspensky as if they were on the same level. This shows a basic ignorance no doubt born of the fact that Amis was never a part of the Fourth Way teaching of Gurdjieff but rather a member of what is called "the main Ouspensky Group" in England.

Therefore, in terms of his direct experience, he can only speak about this particular group. And yet he proposes to speak for the Work in toto when he claims that there has been since Gurdjieff's death only "a mechanical reiteration of his [Gurdjieff's] teachings." He goes even further when he announces that "no comparable teachers [to Gurdjieff] have arisen within that stream."

Never having been part of the mainstream teaching Amis' statement is simply hearsay. Regarding his charge of "mechanical reiteration," one suggests that Amis read Lord Pentland's *Exchanges Within*. As to "no comparable teachers have arisen," we would ask: Is St. Paul comparable with Jesus Christ? In two thousand years Christianity has produced no one who has attained a level comparable to Jesus Christ. (Christians, of course, believe that Jesus was the *one and only* son of God so no one could. But the fact is no one has.)

Looking still deeper at Amis' statement, we see it shows how he is seeing Gurdjieff—simply as a teacher. But Jesus and Gurdjieff were more than teachers. The first reformed a teaching, Judaism, and the second brought an ancient teaching, reformulated for our time. This argument of Amis' is as specious as is his declaration that "nobody, anywhere, speaks today of obtaining results or hoping to obtain results from this 'system'." Amis should be reminded that the teaching is esoteric and matters of consequence are certainly not spoken about openly; this is especially so in terms of results (which reveals a certain unfortunate attitude).

Amis also mentions Ouspensky telling of a missing noetic method. This, Amis says, "actually exists in the prayer of the heart [the Jesus Prayer] used in the inner tradition of the Eastern Church." Amis gives no reference for this remark so it cannot be checked for accuracy and context, but for the sake of discussion let the idea be accepted. To begin with, the record shows that Ouspensky used the Jesus Prayer as early as 1931. J. G. Bennett reported that Ouspensky gave the prayer to his followers. However, said Bennett:

"Within a few weeks of introducing the exercises of memorizing and repetition [of the Sermon on the Mount and the Jesus Prayer], Ouspensky refused to discuss them at his meetings, saying that they had been misunderstood, and, if persisted in would give wrong results." (*Witness,* pp. 163-64.)

If the Jesus Prayer was the missing noetic method, why then did Ouspensky discontinue its use? The alleged misunderstanding could be easily corrected, so why did he not do it? This is not to denigrate the Jesus Prayer in any way, but simply to show that for Ouspensky it was *not* the so-called missing method. Also, it should be noted that Gurdjieff's *First Series* contains many prayers and hymns so that Gurdjieff was well aware of prayer and its uses.

Every important assertion of Amis' falls apart when scrutinized in the light of the written record. The rest is either circumstantial, highly interpretative or depends on sources now dead or who cannot be named. Thus, in the end, we have only to rely on the objectivity of the publisher which, given the foregoing, is not merited.

Finally, and of not very much importance, it should be said that Robin Amis does finally admit that Mouravieff had "a personal dislike of Gurdjieff," one he claims not to share. Fair enough. However, he is doing his best to discredit Gurdjieff and distort the teaching and for this, regrettably, he is altogether responsible. Δ

Appendix IV

Mouravieff and The Secret of The Source

The summer 1991 issue of *Gnosis* magazine, ostensibly devoted to the Gurdjieff work, contains an article by Robin Amis entitled, "Mouravieff and The Secret of the Source." There is enough wrong thinking to bear a refutation. Here are the main points.

1. Amis begins by implying that Ouspensky's *Search* is the main text of the Fourth Way and asks "why was the System only available in fragmentary form, and why are only fragments of the System available today, over seventy years after it was introduced."

First, the Fourth Way is a not a system, though that is how Ouspensky referred to it. As Gurdjieff said quite clearly and Ouspensky recorded: "The teaching whose theory is here being set out...."

That Amis believes that Ouspensky's *Search* represents the teaching and not Gurdjieff's *Legominism* is an error of astounding proportion. It would be like saying that the letters of St. Paul represented Christianity and not the New Testament, had Jesus written it.

Without question and beyond all reasonable argument, Gurdjieff's *All and Everything* represents the teaching. The *First Series* was published in 1949; the *Second Series* in 1963; and the *Third Series* in 1975.

2. Referring to Gurdjieff's saying that "the 'keepers' from whom he received this knowledge 'did not understand it all.'"

I can find no reference of Gurdjieff ever calling the Church fathers *keepers* or his saying he got his knowledge from them. It certainly does not appear in reference in Amis' article to Gurdjieff and Mouravieff speaking at the Café de la Paix (see the Mouravieff section in this book).

3. "But if *understanding* is, as both Gurdjieff and Ouspensky say, an essential element in the System, Gurdjieff's statement implies that he did not receive the System in the form of understanding but as *information*."

As he did not get his knowledge from the Church fathers this statement does not apply to Gurdjieff.

4. "The way of development of hidden possibilities is a way *against Nature, against God.*" Amis speaks of this statement as a denial of God by Gurdjieff. This is a very serious misrepresentation.

To understand how Gurdjieff means this, the reader must know in what way Gurdjieff uses the terms involution and evolution. Involution is the continuing manifestation of life; this is a descending octave as in the Ray of Creation. Evolution is to go against this manifestation, to swim upstream; this is an ascending octave. See Makary

Kronbernkzion's thesis, "The Affirming and Denying Influences on Man," *First Series*, p. 1139.

5. "We can find detailed terminology that makes it incontestable that many of the special terms of the System were fully developed decades before the births of Gurdjieff and Ouspensky....This confirms that the immediate origins of the System lie in certain unwesternized segments of the Russian church."

Here, Amis is speaking of St. Theophan the Recluse. Because of Amis' statement, we have read two books by St. Theophan, *The Heart of Salvation* and *The Spiritual Life and How to be Attuned to It*. In our view, Amis' statement is without justification. (See Appendix IV.)

6. "What was Gurdjieff's goal in fact? Nobody has ever known. It is as difficult to try to deduce this from his acts as it was in the case of Rasputin."—Mouravieff.

Gurdjieff's goal/mission was to establish the ancient teaching of the Fourth Way in the West so the world would not destroy itself.

Mouravieff's linking of Gurdjieff to Rasputin shows that he, like his protégé, will go to any length to try to make a point. This is particularly unconscionable.

7. "Saint Theophan who taught a form of 'self-remembering'."

It is interesting that Amis covers himself here by using the words "form of," for the 'self-remembering' that Theophan speaks of is not what Gurdjieff presented. All religions and ways of development make use of attention, energy and the like. This does not make them one and the same. Saint Theophan's 'self-remembering' is not Gurdjieff's. Δ

Appendix V

Saint Theophan

Saint Theophan the Recluse (1815-1894), canonized as a saint in the Russian Orthodox Church in 1988, was a graduate of Orel Seminary and a teacher at Kiev Theological Academy. For a brief time he was Rector of the Saint Petersburg Theological Academy before becoming bishop of Tambov and later, the city of Vladimir. At the age of fifty-one Theophan resigned his office to enter the monastery of Vysha as an anchorite and, after six years, withdrew to live as a hermit-scholar for the last eighteen years of his life in the monastery of Vysha. Well versed in Greek and possibly Syriac—he made two journeys abroad, once living in Jerusalem for seven years—he led the translation of the *Philokalia* and *Unseen Warfare* from Greek into Russian.

The *Philokalia* is a collection of texts written in Greek by the Fathers of the Church in the fourth and fifth centuries. A selection of texts were translated into liturgical Slavonic and published in Moscow in 1793. In 1857 it was translated from the Slavonic into Russian. In 1877 Theophan, amending, omitting certain passages, and paraphrasing others, added 1,800 additional pages to this five-volume work and produced a new edition.

The *Unseen Warfare* was first written by the Catholic priest Lorenzo Scupoli in 1589 in the form of two texts entitled *Spiritual Combat* and *Path to Paradise*. In the eighteenth century, Nicodemus of the Holy Mountain translated both texts and then combined them under the title *Unseen Warfare*. Theophan made so many changes in order that it might conform to Church doctrine that in his foreword he wrote that the book "should be regarded as a free rendering rather than a literal translation."

In speaking of this, Robin Amis writes that while "its concern for accuracy is very great, [it] is based on the need to give practical instruction, not to preserve a historical record....It is clear that Theophan was never embarrassed when he changed the original text of Scupoli in this way. What cannot be amended is either suppressed or radically transformed—not to fit Theophan's own ideas, but to fit the doctrine of the Fathers and the teaching of scripture."

Amis then makes a characteristic leap of apology and spin, saying, "So what Theophan means by 'free rendering' is actually a conscientious restoration of original doctrine, a far from 'easy option.'" But this 'restoration' has come at the expense of altering the original document to make it conform to Church doctrine, thus opening the question of possible distortion. If the "historical record" mentioned above was merely on the level of dates, names, places and events it would be one thing. But this record is comprised of something far more serious—Father Scupoli's own religious experience and the perspective and interpretation he draws from it. In the light of the foregoing, it is interesting to reconsider Mouravieff's statement in his *Gnosis*, Vol. 1: "The Christian Esoteric Tradition is based on the Canon, the Rites, on the Menaion, and lastly on the Doctrine. The latter is a collection of rules, treatises and commentaries written by the doctors of the ecumenical Church. These texts were in large part assembled in a collection called the *Philokalia* [and also *Unseen Warfare*]."

The point is that these writings to which Mouravieff and Amis so often allude have *not* been passed down through the centuries as (1) a complete whole, and (2) have undergone extensive editings and many alterations, additions, and "free renderings." The intrinsic spiritual merit of these texts is not being questioned. What *is* being questioned is the assertion by Mouravieff and Amis that they represent the Christian esoteric tradition. Δ

Appendix VI

Ouspensky & Christianity

Ouspensky's attraction to Christianity began after he had left Gurdjieff. For in the beginning, he writes that "schools of either a frankly religious nature or a half-religious character...did not attract me." And when he asked Gurdjieff where his companions were and Gurdjieff told him that "some have gone into seclusion" [*cloistered* is used in the original draft], Ouspensky says, "This word from the monastic language, heard so unexpectedly, gave me a strange and uncomfortable feeling." Then in Essentuki when he decided to leave Gurdjieff (for the first time) he said quite bluntly that the religious way which he believed that Gurdjieff was leading his students toward "*is not my way.*" [Ouspensky's italics.]

At some point after leaving Gurdjieff—no doubt trying to find another way—Ouspensky must have
changed his mind about Christianity, for he began to
study it in earnest. Ouspensky's student Maurice Nicoll
gave an interesting picture of this: "Ouspensky has the
New Testament in German, French, Russian and English,
and when he is speaking of a verse he looks at the translation in each of them and in the Greek version."

In the course of his study of Christianity, Ouspensky
made contact with a Father Nikon, a hermit on Mt.
Athos. After Ouspensky's death in 1947, Gerald Palmer
and Madame Kadloubovsky, students of Ouspensky's,
contacted the hermit. This eventually led to their translating parts of the *Philokalia* into English, as well as the
Unseen Warfare.

And in examining Ouspensky's *Search*, a book he
began to write in 1921 and revised until his death
twenty-six years later, we find in the section in which he
is writing about Christianity, a mention of Mount Athos.
There was an exercise, according to Gurdjieff, which
"had been preserved up to our time in the monasteries of
Mount Athos." (Note that Gurdjieff speaks of "an exercise" being preserved, not an esoteric teaching.)

How Ouspensky saw Christianity at the end of his life
is not known, but we do know that shortly before his
death he told Dr. Francis Roles, one of his most senior
students and the man charged with leading Ouspensky's
groups in England after his death—"You must go and
find a method by which to remember yourSelf. If you
find the method you may find the source." This directive
eventually took Roles to India and Advaita Vedanta, not
Mount Athos and Christianity, esoteric or otherwise. Δ

Index

151

Struggle of the Magicians
Exploring the Teacher-Student Relationship

by William Patrick Patterson

Yes, what an excellent book—full of things I didn't know. A real contribution to our understanding of Gurdjieff and Uspenskii."
> —**Colin Wilson**, author,
> *The War Against Sleep*

Struggle of the Magicians will fascinate anyone interested in the Fourth Way. I could hardly put it down."
> —**Charles T. Tart**, Ph.D., Prof. Psychology, UC Davis; author, *Waking Up*

"For many of us, Gurdjieff and Uspenskii have remained mysteriously attractive but dauntingly difficult to grasp. *Struggle of the Magicians* is a hard to put down' exception to much of the literature available about Gurdjieff, presenting his life and work almost like a play against the panoramic backdrop of his turbulent times, from World War I and the Russian Revolution through World War II."
> —*Light on Consciousness* Magazine

Struggle of the Magicians is an important contribution to the history of alternative spirituality in the West. The tension between the richly contrasting personalities of Gurdjieff and Uspenskii is a cameo of the problems with which the personal transformation tradition has had to contend, while at the same time their story illumines in real life context the powerful vistas its visions have opened. It is the finely-told chronicle of a classic event in occult history, set against the backdrop of overwhelmingly dramatic historical events, effectively set into the narrative as datelines.
> —**Robert S. Ellwood**, Chairman, Dept. of Religious Studies University of Southern California

Struggle of the Magicians is available at all serious bookstores.

Or write the publisher: Arete Communications, 773 Center Boulevard #58, Fairfax, CA 94978-0058; Fax: (510) 848-0159. Add $3.50 for postage within continental U.S.A. Outside, add $9.00 for surface; $14 for air mail.

Second Edition. 5.5 x 8.5. 336 pp. Acid-Free Paper. Bibliography and Index. Softcover. ISBN: 1-879514-80-8. $19.95.

Distributors: *Partners, Bookpeople, New Leaf, Samuel Weiser, Baker & Taylor.* In Australia: *Banyan Tree*, P.O. Box 269, Stirling 5152, South Australia. In Europe: *Golden Square Books*, 16 The Village Golden Square, London, WIR 3AG, England.

Excerpts from
Struggle of the Magicians

Part II: Magicians at War

DECEMBER 1, 1921. LONDON. "Uspenskii seemed rather depressed when I last saw him," says Rosamund Bland, "and talked of going away, back to Constantinople, because things were not going well here. As far as I can make out he thinks I am the only one who takes things really seriously and who can be of use to the work from his point of view, and it is not worth his while to spend so much energy in order to perhaps get one person into a condition where they can be useful. If he is going to spend so much force, he must have more result than that."

EARLY FEBRUARY 1922. LONDON. Six months after Gurdjieff's arrival in the West, his Institute for the Harmonious Development of Man remains only an idea. Hearing of Uspenskii's success, the fate of these two men ever entwined, Gurdjieff crosses the Channel. They meet and Uspenskii's attitude becomes "much more definite." He sees again, so he believes, "all the former obstacles that had begun to appear in Essentuki." He doesn't believe it's possible to work with Gurdjieff. Yet, still he expects "a great deal more from Gurdjieff's work." And so he doesn't break entirely. In fact, Uspenskii decides to help Gurdjieff establish his Institute in London.

FEBRUARY 13, 1922. LONDON. Gurdjieff's first talk[1] in London is at the Theosophical Hall at Warwick Gardens. Some sixty people attend. Many, including Orage, already think of themselves as Uspenskii's pupils.

---

1. The exact number of meetings in London and the dates on which they were held remain uncertain, given the references in the public sources from that period.

Gurdjieff and his translators, Major Frank Pinder and Olga de Hartmann, along with Uspenskii, mount the platform. The audience, awed by Gurdjieff's presence, sits in petrified silence. Gurdjieff, as always, comes right to the point:

"When we speak of ourselves ordinarily we speak of 'I.' We say *'I' did this...'I' think this...'I' want to do this*— but this is a mistake. There is no such 'I' or rather there are hundreds, thousands of little 'I's in every one of us....We are governed by external circumstances. All our actions follow the line of least resistance to the pressure of outside circumstances."

Gurdjieff is asked if it is possible to alter one's emotions through acts of judgment.

"One center of our machine cannot change another center," he answers. "For example: in London I am irritable, the weather and the climate dispirit me and make me bad-tempered whereas in India I am good-tempered. Therefore my judgment tells me to go to India and I shall drive out the emotion of irritability. But then, in London, I find I can work; in the tropics not as well. And so, there I should be irritable for another reason. You see, emotions exist independently of the judgment and you cannot alter one by means of another."

"Mr. Gurdjieff, what would it be like to be conscious in essence?"

"Everything more vivid," is Gurdjieff's memorable, rapier-like reply.

After this first talk, there is no question of who is teacher, who the student for one member of the audience. "I *knew* that Gurdjieff was the teacher," declares Orage. "Uspenskii for me represented knowledge—great knowledge; Gurdjieff, understanding—though of course Gurdjieff had all the knowledge, too."

MARCH 5, 1922. LONDON. Gurdjieff returns from Germany to give a second talk and takes questions. Frank

Pinder is translating. At its close he chastises his audience:

"All the questions I have heard tonight are higher mathematics. Nobody knows elementary mathematics.[2] And so such questions are useless."

Later, in speaking privately with Uspenskii, he finally delivers an all-out assault.

He was working on the wrong lines, Gurdjieff told him. He was too intellectual. He lacked an understanding of the real purpose of the Work and of Gurdjieff himself. All his vast knowledge would be useless, he told him, unless he worked on himself in order to understand basic principles. If he truly wished to understand, he must stop teaching and begin again—work again with Gurdjieff.

It is a scorching appraisal. How could Uspenskii not hear it? Not understand his identification? Believe that he was a spiritual equal, or near-equal, to Gurdjieff? Given that Uspenskii is a man of rare intellect, honest and uncompromising in his search for real knowledge, his blindness here and elsewhere shows the strength of buffers.[3] But Uspenskii didn't hear the appraisal—he heard the assault.

MARCH 15, 1922. LONDON. Failing to awaken his rebellious pupil privately, Gurdjieff plays one of his last cards. He gives still another talk at Warwick Gardens, this time on the theme of "Essence and Personality." Instead of Uspenskii, Gurdjieff has Frank Pinder translate.

"Normal human beings are the exception. Nearly everyone has only the essence of a child. It is not natural that in a grown-up man the essence should be a child. Because of this, he remains timid underneath and full of

2. This is a subtle criticism of Uspenskii who is a mathematician.

3. Psychological 'partitions' created to lessen shocks and contradictions so that "a man can always be in the right." See *Search*, pp. 154–55.

apprehensions. This is because he knows that he is not what he pretends to be, but he cannot understand why."

Uspenskii suddenly breaks in, saying that Pinder's translation is not accurate. "Pinder is interpreting for me—not you," answers Gurdjieff.

He then directly attacks Uspenskii, repeating in public now what had been said in private: *Uspenskii is neither mandated nor qualified to teach....*[4]

Later, Gurdjieff remarks to Pinder of the meeting: "Now they will *have* to choose a teacher." Presumably, Uspenskii will have to as well: either himself or Gurdjieff. But for all of Gurdjieff's words and the enormity of his presence, they are without effect. Uspenskii continues to believe in his conclusions. Yet, despite the anger and betrayal he must have felt, he still doesn't break completely with Gurdjieff. In fact, he helps to collect money for Gurdjieff's London Institute. But he does say unequivocally—"I had decided for myself that if the Institute opened in London I would go either to Paris or to America."

And so, as it has openly continued since Uspenskii first broke with Gurdjieff in Essentuki, the struggle between the two continues.[5] The Institute finally opens but Gurdjieff, though the Home Secretary agrees he is no Bolshevik, has a visa problem. Lady Rothermere says she will attempt to wield her influence. But to no avail. Gurdjieff's visa denied, the Institute closes.

---

4. It is a brutal disrobing. Uspenskii, the pupil Gurdjieff had staked his hopes upon to help him establish his teaching, takes himself to be awake. Uspenskii believes he is able to judge his teacher's motives, his character, and yet Uspenskii had still not worked on essence. His development is only partial. To continue to teach would crystallize him at a level that would make further development impossible. So though the verbal assault is brutal, it is necessary.

5.   Though never mentioned by either, it seems reasonable to conclude the struggle, given Uspenskii's experience in Finland, occurs on both the physical and "astral" planes.

Uspenskii's old love, Anna Ilinishna Butkovsky-Hewitt, and he meet in London. Anna is disturbed by the change in him. "He had developed a hard outer shell," she says, "and I wondered then why he had crushed the gentle, poetic radiance of his Petersburg days. Possibly he thought of this side of himself as a weakness, yet it was in this happy mood that his inspiration and vision were strongest: the intellect had nothing to do with it."

JULY 14, 1922. PARIS. With Germany inhospitable to Gurdjieff's Institute and the English door shut, France becomes the choice by default. Gurdjieff arrives from Germany accompanied by the de Hartmanns. They are met by the de Salzmanns.

Soon it is learned that a beautifully furnished château is available at Fontainebleau, forty-four miles from Paris. It is the property of the widow of Fernand Labori, the lawyer who successfully defended Captain Dreyfus, who had been accused of spying. Called the Prieuré des Basses Loges, it has an interesting history, having once been a Carmelite Monastery and, earlier, the home of Louis XIV's famous mistress, Madame de Maintenon.

The château sits behind a high stone wall and heavy iron gates, and, it has not been lived in since 1914. A small fountain lies within the gates of the two-story château; to the rear is a terrace with two more fountains and a long avenue of lime, maple, chestnut, and conifer trees. In the gardens there are an enormous glass orangery, a small house in the gardens known as "Le Paradou," and other outbuildings. The château is set in a park of forty-five acres. An additional 200 acres, bounded by a stone wall, adjoin the Forest of Fontainebleau.

After some strong negotiating by Olga de Hartmann— Gurdjieff told her to remember herself at all times and never to forget her intention—the château is leased, fully furnished, for 65,000 francs with an option to buy for 700,000 francs.

AUGUST 30, 1922. LONDON. Orage tells his friend, the New Zealand short story writer Katherine Mansfield, near death from tuberculosis, about Uspenskii. She begins to attend Uspenskii's lectures. Her husband, John Middleton Murray, does as well, but he is not impressed. "I don't *feel* influenced by Uspenskii....I merely feel I've heard ideas like my ideas, but bigger ones, far more definite ones."

SEPTEMBER 30, 1922. PRIEURÉ. One year after his arrival in the West, Gurdjieff's Institute is established. It will be set up on the same basis as before, that is, "I wished to create around myself conditions in which man would be continually reminded of the sense and aim of his existence by an unavoidable friction between his conscience and the automatic manifestations of his nature." Funds for the Institute—"This child I had conceived," says Gurdjieff—are supplied by the English, notably Mary Lilian, Lady Rothermere, and Ralph Philipson, a Northumberland coal mine owner.

A prospectus for the Institute is written and circulated. It begins:

The Institute for the Harmonious Development of Man by means of the system of Gurdjieff is, as it were, the continuation of the society known as the Seekers After Truth....

The prospectus continues with a short history of the society and then begins its analysis of the conditions and situation which faces modern man, who, it says, has become "an uprooted being, unable to adapt to his life, alien to all its present conditions." It shows where the problems lie and tells how the Institute will help its students to correct them.

MID-OCTOBER 1922. PRIEURÉ. Though the Institute does not officially open until November, Katherine Mansfield arrives. She has become convinced that Gurdjieff could not only help her with her disease but with a spiritual regeneration as well. Though it is obvious she has not long to live, Gurdjieff allows her to stay.

Her letters[6] give a feeling for what is taking place:

It's a most wonderful old place in an amazingly lovely park. About forty people, chiefly Russians, are here working, at every possible kind of thing—I mean outdoor work, looking after animals, gardening, indoor work, music, dancing—it seems a bit of everything....A dancing hall is being built and the house is still being organized....Mr. Gurdjieff likes me to go into the kitchen in the late afternoon and 'watch.' I have a chair in a corner. It's a large kitchen with six helpers—Madame Ostrovsky [Ostrowska], the head [Gurdjieff's wife], walks about like a queen exactly—she is extremely beautiful. Mr. Gurdjieff strides in, takes up a handful of shredded cabbage and eats it...there are at least twenty pots on the stove—and it's so full of life and humor and ease that one wouldn't be anywhere else....The cows are being bought today—Gurdjieff is going to build a high couch in the stable where I can sit and inhale their breath! I know later on I shall be put in charge of those cows—Everyone calls them already 'Mrs. Murray's cows.' Δ

6. According to Gurdjieff, only the constant sensing and knowledge of the inevitability of one's own death, as well as the death of everyone around us, can destroy the egoism that has swallowed up our essence. Katherine Mansfield's last letters stand as a testament to the working of this realization. They reflect the work she did on herself and the understanding she came to in so short a time.

Eating The "I":
A Direct Account
of The Fourth Way—
The Way of Self-Transformation
in Ordinary Life

by William Patrick Patterson

"Most books on the Work, while quite valuable, are too dry. *Eating The "I"* is a major step in changing that: here we have a real human being, like you and I, struggling with Gurdjieff's teachings, sharing moments of despair and moments of insight and liberation."

—Charles T. Tart, Ph. D.
Author of *Waking Up*

"*Eating The "I"* gives as full a picture of the Work as it may be possible to get without joining it. The book comes from a great depth and carries much conviction." — *Gnosis*

"Patterson has two fine Irish gifts: a vivid memory and a storyteller's ear. Paced like a novel and filled with colorful characters, this spiritual autobiography is certain to appeal to those who want a rare and engaging inside glimpse of the Gurdjieff Work." — *Yoga Journal*

"Patterson's work is in a class with Christopher Isherwood's devastatingly frank, and brilliant, story of his spiritual quest, *My Guru and his Disciple*. Writers in the Gurdjieff tradition tend to do autobiography. There are the classic accounts of life with Mr. Gurdjieff by Ouspensky, de Hartmann, Peters and others. *Eating The "I"* will find an honored place in that series."

—Robert S. Ellwood, Chairman, Dept. of Religious Studies
University of Southern California

Eating The "I" is available at all serious bookstores.

Or write the publisher: Arete Communications, 773 Center Boulevard #58, Fairfax, CA 94978-0058; Fax: (510) 848-0159. Add $3.50 for postage within continental U.S.A. Outside, add $9.00 for surface; $14 for air mail.

Four-color cover. 6 x 9. 370 pp. Acid-Free Paper. Bibliography. Softcover. ISBN: 1-879514-77-X. $19.95.

Distributors: *Partners, Bookpeople, New Leaf, Samuel Weiser, Baker & Taylor*. In Australia: *Banyan Tree*, P.O. Box 269, Stirling 5152, South Australia. In Europe: *Golden Square Books*, 16 The Village Golden Square, London, WIR 3AG, England.

Excerpts from
Eating The "I"

Prologue

I HAD BEEN IN THE WORK ONLY A SHORT TIME WHEN JOHN Pentland, my teacher, told me, "Perhaps someday you'll write a book about The Fourth Way—the way of transformation in life." His words went in like a sword. Now, some twenty years after receiving this task, that sword is coming out of the stone.

With the recent passing of Madame Jeanne de Salzmann, Gurdjieff's personal secretary and, since his death in 1949, the leader of the worldwide Work, most of Gurdjieff's direct students are gone. A few have left accounts of their experiences with Gurdjieff and their understanding of the teaching he brought at so great a cost. The book you hold now comes from a different place in the octave of the teaching. For my generation, like all succeeding, can commonly encounter Gurdjieff only through his books. Yet his spirit lives on in the powerful ideas and practices of the Work. But, effectively, what matters is not how close or remote one is to Gurdjieff in terms of ordinary time, but how sincere and persistent is the search.

The intent here is to give a direct and unvarnished account of my years in an esoteric school of The Fourth Way. My interest is in the collision that occurs between the teaching and the "I," the conditioned self-identity. This meeting is ancient and archetypal, an evoked alchemy between the impersonal and personal; the objective and subjective. My aim is to portray the wonder and misunderstanding, the discovery and resistance, that marks the seed of this potentiality for a new life.

Eating The "I" is a story of my struggle with ignorance and arrogance, the friction between the desires and the non-desires, that led to many suffered truths and some hard-won understanding, all coming under the masterful teaching and example of the remarkable man who Gurdjieff chose to lead the Work in America, Lord John Pentland.

In writing of my search, I made a compact with myself: I would invent nothing—I would tell the story exactly as I experienced it. The reason is both simple and beautiful. Life needs no invention. So-called ordinary life is extraordinary when I pay attention. Free attention frees the moment. Impressions once static are now dynamic, multidimensional. The moment expands. The physical "becomes" the metaphysical. The symbolic and mythological come into play. The dance begins. Do I identify? Through hard experience I learn that, though rarefied, the symbolic, the mythological, are still content, still things. Beyond them lie emptiness, silence, real I. Awakening to the elegance of this truth, I see the work is not to change myself, but my vibration. In certain places, then, to reflect this change in fluidity and inclusiveness, tenses are changed.

This book is not, nor is it intended to be—a "pure" reflection of the Work. The aim instead is to give an intimate report of how I worked and did not work with the ideas. And how, too, they influenced and inspired me and, yes, how they tore me, the "I," apart. I have not painted any sparrows yellow, nor otherwise gilded my idiocy. It should be noted, however, that there is a "mixing" of ideas here. This is because of my attraction to not only the ideas of Gurdjieff, but also those of Jung, Heidegger and certain others. So read with a critical eye.

There is, of course, concern about publishing an intimate work on the esoteric. Gurdjieff's teaching is not for everyone. Nor should it be. The Esoteric Tradition is just that: esoteric. Without the material necessary to understand in Gurdjieff's sense the relativity of the scale of vibration, recognition of this fact is not commonly possible. Gurdjieff took great pains to "bury the bones," to guard against the teaching falling into unprepared or profane hands. As is well-known: when the esoteric is made exoteric, when real knowledge is bought too cheaply—a lawful deflection and distortion must result. Once again then we witness the spectre, too common to our time, of a once sacred channel giving only ordinary tap water. Let us keep in mind, as well, what Rene´ Guénon wrote in his masterwork *The Reign of Quantity*:

> *Every truth of a transcendent order necessarily partakes*
> *of the inexpressible; it is essentially in this fact that the*
> *profound significance of the initiatic secret really lies; no*
> *kind of exterior secret can ever have any value except as an*
> *image or symbol of the initiatic secret... But it must be*
> *understood that these are things of which the meaning and*
> *the range are completely lost to the modern mentality, and*
> *incomprehension of them quite naturally engenders hostility;*
> *besides the ordinary man always has an instinctive fear of what*
> *he does not understand and fear engenders hatred only too easily.*

Perhaps a warning is also in order. Namely, that to practice any of the ideas mentioned herein, independent of the inner knowledge and objective pressure that only an authentic teacher and school can apply, will only cement the person further into his or her most cherished "I"; and so produce yet another instance of the ego burying the essence alive, the true "living death."

My wish and intent here is to walk the razor's edge between the exoteric and esoteric, casting a little sacrificial human flesh into the public fires as payment. In striving to fulfill the task given to me over twenty years ago, I must of necessity put my "I" on display. It might just as well be anyone's fixed idea of themselves. Idiots are idiots. The heart of the matter lies in the essential collision of worlds, that of the timeless with the temporal, and That which remains ever the same. This account describes, then, what it is like to voluntarily undergo the unorthodox and uncompromising spiritual discipline of the mainstream school, yet ever honors its hidden core and tradition.

Chapter 1
A Son's Search
(Excerpt)

AT THIS TIME OF EVENING THE RCA BUILDING SEEMED like a massive burial tomb. Inside it was cool, dark and silent, bereft of people, save for a few grizzled guards whiling away the time. I took the elevator to his floor and slowly made my way down the dimly lighted corridor, the only sound was that of my soles squeaking on the marble floor. Finally, I came to a door reading:
John Pentland
The American-British Electric Corporation
The Hunting Group of Companies
I knocked several times. I expected to meet a portly and dour English gentleman wearing a vest and a gold watch chain. He'd have jowls, wear glasses. Perhaps have a crop of white hair. No answer. I waited. The office was dark. Empty. I cursed. Had he forgotten? Was he playing a trick? I was about to leave when, on impulse, I tried the brass door knob. It clicked. The door opened. The light was faint, ghostly, the office painted in shadows

and blackness. I felt like a burglar. An ordinary business office. On the walls were large geological and topographical maps. I glanced at some papers on a desk. This "Lord Pentland" was the company's president.

I was about to leave when I heard the sound of a door opening. I took a few furtive steps forward and peered down a long corridor. In the pale light I saw a tall silent figure, very erect, slender, moving through the shadows toward me. He seemed like some prehistoric bird. He was upon me almost before I knew it. The face was totally impassive. The eyes aware. Yet without expression. The neck was very long, reed-like. It seemed too slender for the head. The eyebrows were dark and bushy. The shoulders were broad. He was balding.

"Hello," I said feigning cheeriness.

No greeting, no response. It was as if I hadn't said anything.

Weird. The two of us, strangers, standing in a dark hallway, half our faces in shadow, and him just standing there. He regarded me impersonally and without the slightest embarrassment. I felt as if he was drinking me in, weighing me in some way. What an odd duck! I could see him as perhaps the abbot of some distant, time-forgotten monastery—but hardly a disciple of a man like Gurdjieff. No, he must be just a caretaker. The teaching must have died with Gurdjieff.

Finally, the eyes and face still without expression, his lips formed a smile. In a low voice, just above a whisper, he said:

"Would you follow me?" A long arm motioned me down the corridor.

We walked down the dusky hallway; the only sounds in my ears were the soft pad of his slippers and the squeak of my shoes. His office was large and ordinary, a little sparse. Without ornamentation. No exotic souvenirs of travels with the Seekers of Truth. No secret symbols of knowledge. Only a few framed family photos. The view was impressive. St. Patrick's Cathedral, Saks, the traffic and crowds along Fifth Avenue, the Manhattan skyline, the bridge to New Jersey. I turned from the bank of windows. He had brought a chair to the side of his desk.

"Sit wherever you like," he said, half-motioning me to a chair by his desk.

Deliberately, I took a chair in front of the windows. He noted that, then took a seat opposite me on a small couch against the wall. His look was as impassive as it had been in the hallway. I took him in now as well. I noticed his ears. They were large, without lobes, nearly coming to a point at the top. Rather elfin-like. This "Lord" wasn't much of a dresser, even for a businessman. He wore charcoal trousers, baggy and beltless, an old dull pea green cardigan, white business shirt, a nondescript wool tie. The dress of a professor of archeology, a scientist maybe. Hardly the stuff of a sly, swashbuckling man like Gurdjieff.

We continued looking at one another. We hadn't sat long when the last rays of the day's sun streamed into my eyes forcing me to move my chair. I was glad for the excuse to move. I thought that might break this awful silence but he continued watching me. I felt like a bug under a microscope. There was something unnerving about him. I sensed he wasn't there in some way. At least not the way I was; the way normal people are. Was he playing some game? I vowed not to speak before he did. Just then he spoke:

"Why have you come?" His voice was soft, unhurried, almost indifferent.

The same question as on the telephone. Again, I felt the same doubt, same bewilderment. *Why* was I there? *What* did I want? *What* had brought me here? I had no answers. I began talking, rambling on, telling him of my early life, how my parents had spoiled me, treating me like a rich kid, buying me anything I ever wanted.

"Well, at least," I said, "it made me realize that material things couldn't make you happy and then, too, death took it all away, so what was the meaning of it all?"

He went on listening

I recounted how I'd studied psychology and philosophy and found no answer with either. Just mind games. Religion seemed too ordinary, played out, and you had to accept its answers on faith.

He made no comment.

"I don't know what life is about," I told him, "but something in me just can't accept that it is all meaningless—there has to be some reason for human life."

I thought he might respond, but he didn't. I waited. He motioned that I should continue.

I told him, too, how after college I'd gone to San Francisco to work in advertising, but was drafted into the Army. Afterward, I'd come to New York. Worked as a copywriter for Montgomery Wards. Later for J. Walter Thompson and BBD&O. Finally ended up at IBM. I told him about how I had started *In New York*, its success, then about the fast buck boys.

Like a broken water main, the whole story burst out of me. I must have talked for a good hour. But he listened, however long and convoluted. He had an amazing ability to listening. He gave no sign of how he felt. Perhaps he only appeared to follow. I couldn't tell. When I got to my theories of what life might be about, its purpose and meaning and all, well, I did notice he seemed to tire visibly. He was in his sixties. Probably had a long day.

I ended by telling him of my spiritual experiences, the light and the telepathy, the inner knowing. I was just getting to the good part when—unbelievably:

He yawned!

Right in my face. No attempt to cover his mouth. No, "excuse me." Not the least embarrassment. He acted as if nothing had happened. Perhaps the "Lord" was a bit senile? Was this another Murphy deal? A wild goose chase? Gurdjieff had died in 1949. This old gaffer—was he just a museum piece?

I hurried then to the end of the story. I was about to excuse myself and leave when—the bastard yawned again!

It was the most incredible yawn I had ever seen. The mouth opened wide, showing a huge cave of teeth and tongue. The neck muscles and tendons stretched full out. Then a loud sucking in of air and the mouth clapped shut, the nostrils exhaling a stream of spent air. The whole mechanical movement of the musculature happened in slow motion, like it was all under his control. He kept his eyes on mine the entire time. They showed nothing. Not the least guilt or apology. Was all this deliberate? If so, why?

I wanted to get the hell out of there, fast. But I didn't. I thought of moving, but couldn't. The thought wasn't strong enough. So we just sat, wrapped in all that heavy silence, all that empty space. It was withering.

"Tell me..." he inquired, feigning a curiosity, "can you experience all that now?"

There was a slight undertone of challenge in his voice. I saw immediately what he meant: I'd talked about my "spiritual experiences" as if they were a continuing part of my life. I felt like a fish with a hook in its mouth.

"No," I finally admitted, a bit reluctantly.

He nodded, acknowledging the truth of my admission.

"But I could then," I added tersely.

"Can you do this now?" He wasn't going to let me off the hook.

I looked out the window. The Manhattan skyline stood in sharp black silhouette against the graying twilight. The lights in the buildings, all yellow—they seemed like thousands of impenetrable cat eyes. What was his point? What was he trying to prove? That I was an idiot?

"No," I finally said somewhat sheepishly, "I can't do it now."

"That's true," he shot back quickly.

It was as if we had come to something now, something important. His voice was so direct, sharp, not whispery at all. And the way he pronounced the word "true"—the elongated tail he put on the 'rue'—flashed right through me. Was he suggesting everything I'd said up to that moment wasn't true? Or only half-true? That only my admission—that *I couldn't do it now*—was worth anything?

The chair felt uncomfortable, unforgiving. I shifted in it uneasily, crossing my legs, clasping my hands around my knee, leaning forward. He shifted as well. More hard silence. I had the most unusual feeling then. It was like a "double feeling." It was as if I was lying and telling the truth—and at the same time.

But everything I'd told him was true! It had happened. I wasn't making it up. So why this feeling of lying? Mentally, I kept seeing reruns of my actions, my words rebounding on me. It was as if I was in some kind of instant replay.

Then his original question—*Why have you come?*— bubbled up in me again.

Suddenly I understood. I hadn't answered his question. I hadn't admitted I didn't know why.

That unlocked something. For immediately I remembered what had brought me—what I wanted. Why had I forgotten?

"I want to become conscious," I told him, another tone in my voice.

Something happened in the room then. There was a shift of some type. Same room, same two people, yet it was all different. I felt the space growing, getting larger and larger, like an invisible balloon expanding. The sense of time changed. It was as if time "thinned out." Δ

EXPLORE TELOS

If the ideas and perspectives of the Fourth Way teaching are of interest, explore *Telos*.

The sole focus of *Telos* is inquiry into self-transformation in our contemporary world. An international twenty-eight-page quarterly, *Telos* publishes interviews, essays, book excerpts, and book and film reviews. It does not, and will not, carry advertising. For its publication, it relies solely on the support of its readership.

If you would like a complimentary copy, please send the enclosed postcard, or write:

Telos
773 Center Boulevard, Box 58
Fairfax, California 94978-0058

E-mail: Telos9@aol.com
Website:
members.aol.com/Telos9

WILLIAM PATRICK PATTERSON
BIOGRAPHY

A longtime student of John Pentland, the man Gurdjieff chose to lead the Work in America, Mr. Patterson has actively practiced the principles of the teaching for over twenty-five years. He is the founder and editor of *Telos*, the first international quarterly devoted to the Fourth Way. A seasoned public speaker, Mr. Patterson regularly lectures on transformational themes, leads seminars, and conducts applied research.

For many years he worked as an editor in publishing and advertising in New York City, and later in Silicon Valley and San Francisco. His work in journalism won many awards including the Jesse H. Neal Award, considered the Pulitzer Prize of business press journalism. While in New York, he founded and edited his own magazine, *In New York*. He lives in a small town in Northern California with his wife and two sons. An avid traveller, he has visited Egypt, Israel, Greece, Turkey, India, Ireland, England, Mexico and Japan, as well as Europe and Scandinavia. He looks forward to visiting Antarctica.